STUDENT EXAM PASSPORT

STUDENT EXAM PASSPORT

Samson Yung-Abu

Library of Congress Control Number:		2019903835
ISBN:	Hardcover	978-1-5434-9396-2
	Softcover	978-1-5434-9395-5
	eBook	978-1-5434-9394-8

Print information available on the last page.

Rev. date: 04/01/2019

To order additional copies of this book, contact:
Xlibris
800-056-3182
www.Xlibrispublishing.co.uk
Orders@Xlibrispublishing.co.uk
789818

Dedicated to Gracie Yung-Abu

A daughter who is always eager to learn and grow. One who makes learning a process of progress, pleasure, and play.

Seek Education

Everything comes and goes in life at some point—the instability of life by nature—but a degree does not. It is like a birth certificate; whether you turn out to be a good kid or a bad kid at the end of your lifespan, it remains there. Whether you have a good job or a bad job, it remains there. Whether you develop an illness or maintain good health, it remains there. It stays, forever, yours for the keeping.

—MSc Samson Yung-Abu

A Student's Role in Education

Education is conclusively about history, evolution, and revolution that needs to maintain survival through each century, through each student. For without students, the survival of education cannot be accounted for, maintained, progressed, or carried on. Without students, education will become static or completely extinct along with human purpose, human progress, and human connection.

—MSc Samson Yung-Abu

CONTENTS

PREFACE

Every transition has a genesis that gives us a
sense of gratitude when we reflect on where we
once were and where we are right now.

There is something intensely gratifying about studying in three different worlds, three different cultures: climate, nurture, and environment. The outcome is that you develop a distinct sense of evolution, growth, value, sustainability, substance, accountability, contribution, stability, significance, and command, as well as control over your future grades and career.

I take myself back to fifteen years ago, coming from a country where the educational system was more primitive, less functional, and less prime. I never thought I would get to this point in my academic life, hungry for more knowledge and wanting to give back. My very first day in a Western classroom felt different, both in structure and in content. I was feeling a fizzy mixture of fear and courage. After a while of sitting and absorbing the scenery in front of me, I felt a sense of excitement.

The atmosphere felt relaxed and calm, with a hint of academic freedom hovering in the air. The teacher was smartly dressed, with sleeves rolled up in a businesslike way and a warm smile—a smile of comfort, enrichment of knowledge, competence, and acceptance. On my fellow students' faces, I could see vivid signs of ambition, composure, confidence, intellectuality, individuality, and smartness. Then, like lightning, it hit me that I would have to put in a rigorous amount of effort to catch up: to be as composed as them, as confident as them, as intelligent and as smart as them. To achieve that, I would have to compete to excel and, as far-fetched as it sounded then, exceed their efforts.

Today, the transition feels like a trip into an advanced and brighter future, one that was unimaginable until it happened. It was like moving from eighties movies straight into twenty-first-century movies. I never thought I could acquire the opportunity to excel like I have today.

It is true, as Malcolm X puts it, that "Education is the passport to the future, for tomorrow belongs to those who prepare for it today." Moreover, while education is indeed the passport to the future, its mobility depends on showing competence in various academic areas. To prepare for the future, one has to get through multiple educational stages: primary school, secondary school, six forms, college, undergraduate, postgraduate, and so on.

This event has enabled me to develop a distinct comparison of and appreciation for how education can evolve the human mind. Many take this for granted. Today, this still baffles me, and I keep asking myself these questions: *How did I get to this stage in my academic and professional career? How did I keep a continuous and determined level of engagement with education? What was the drive, the motive, the logic, the impetus that led to a master's degree and the tutoring of different level of students?*

I started out in a primitive educational environment where we had to bring our own desks and chairs to school (heavy timbers in hot weather conditions in Africa). I walked for miles—an hour to school and another hour back—to sit in a classroom with no walls, no physical windows, and at times, no seats (we connected wooden planks together to sit on and listen to the teaching). Today, I sit comfortably while I listen to the teaching in a nice well-furnished classroom conducive to learning. The lecture rooms have brick and glass walls and are occupied by distinctive teachers, projecting an atmosphere of taste, sophistication, assurance, modernity, and diligent care. The classroom is equipped with windows, air-conditioning, microphones, the latest gadgets, various student accessories, and the newest technologies. Being part of this newness and enveloped in it, I consistently feel like a kid in a candy shop, each day in every class.

In recent years, I realised that my drive in constantly seeking knowledge was for becoming two people in one: a better student and a better person through knowledge and understanding, all of which are now readily available in abundance. To become that student and person, I had to get through each academic stage by passing all required exams. This was hard for me, because coming from a different country meant that I had to do more than others. I had a gap in knowledge. I had to consistently seek to catch up to the others, to keep up with the others, and to go beyond the average student in an effort to excel.

The gap in knowledge was a constant reminder on my college review. Luckily, the teachers never stopped believing that I could do better, that I *would* do better. They wrote that I just needed to concentrate more, pay attention more, and study harder and more consistently. Then I got the picture, and I knew what I needed to do. I began the journey that landed me where I am today and led me to write this book.

It is undoubtedly the case that to get through the academic stages into the future that we want to belong in, we have to prepare for exams. This book is highly recommended for students who are determined to end the academic year with a better outlook on exam-taking and become a better person in the process. A student who gets consistently high grades in exams is considered to have shown distinction in understanding and the application of knowledge in a disciplined fashion. These students continuously produce exceptionality because they have practiced it and displayed their knowledge in a compelling and distinctive style.

The chapters in this book will unfold the knowledge and understanding students need to show the level of competence required to be top of the class, to be confident exam-takers, to predict specific problems, and to extinguish those problems before they develop. This book is packed with knowledge capable of providing students with a profound ability to show consistency in the grades they wish to produce.

Taking an exam can be unsettling and overwhelming. This is partly because, at some point during our academic lives, understanding becomes more crucial than intelligence. Studying around the clock, napping in the library, straining our eyesight, ignoring leisure time, and avoiding sleep while trying to cram months' worth of teaching into a few days and nights won't do the trick. Those days have left us. At best, this behaviour only prolongs the inevitable (including stress, failure, regrets, and disengagement).

I first wrote this book before my final two exams and published it. At some point after its publication, I was uncertain as to whether I had published it out of bravery or out of confidence that I would pass my exams or perhaps both. But publish it I did, and it drove me to work harder and smarter to achieve exceptional and consistent grades.

The days when I had to use a shady old worn-out lantern with little kerosene to study in the dark while ignoring or extinguishing mosquitoes are over. Today, I have a real study lights, a real study desk, authentic study materials, no mosquitoes to distract me, and my *Student Exam Passport* to guide me. I have no excuses, and when I narrow my thoughts, I still can't find any.

Now, sitting in a room with other intellectuals dressed in their best suits, shirts, dresses, and shoes, all looking formal, I am reassured that I invested well in knowing what there is to know about how to learn—all the little details and understanding we must inscribe in our student minds to attain our desired grades. I didn't just get my money's worth throughout the process, which some folks expect to be the sole purpose of attending educational institutions. I got more: I got my future's worth, my career's worth, a dream's worth. It has been a priceless encounter.

Acknowledgements

No matter who we have become or who we have failed to become—no matter where we have come from or where we are heading to, or where we have got to or where we never arrived at but hoped to be—we've never ever walked a path alone. We have always had a body, a soul, a heart, a life, a significant presence, a companion around us who deserves at the very least a special thank you. And for this particular reason, I am deeply grateful to my readers and supporters. Thank you all.

Education has played a dominant role in my life journey, and I have a lot of folks and institutions to thank—even countries. Without them, this book would never have materialised. Neither would my knowledge and awareness of the power of education in the fast-paced and creative twenty-first-century world we all live in.

The publication of this book is inspired by my learning journey in Nigeria, Germany, and the United Kingdom. Its publication is inevitable, because I have lived and been schooled in these three distinct countries, in which there has been a constant challenge to learn, adjust, and adapt. I have had to learn with more focus, more determination, more motivation, and a genuine interest to compete.

At times, the journey was overwhelmingly hard and rough, filled with potholes of doubt, wrinkled with tedious demands, clayed with confusion—a restless, endless challenge to stay current among my peers. Other times, the journey was less challenging and subtle, filled with joyful results and fruitful adventures and experience that money can't genuinely buy. The best thing about it all was that during those hard times, I did what I do best. I remained focused and determined, because I know that like everything else, the potholes eventually get filled up, the wrinkles get ironed out with the right pressure, and the challenges come to an end.

The truth is, as students, we crave achievement, clarity, accuracy, expertise, and opportunity. We turn to education for answers, directions, instructions, and awareness. Education is a sequence of consequences—an act which in hindsight justifies its value if applied rightfully. I remember the days when I had to study for various exams with candles and lanterns and use them sparingly, with moths and mosquitos circling the light and baiting me with distraction.

I still cherish those days, but believe me, my choice of lighting was not because studying by candlelight was colourful or romantic. Back then, candles or lanterns were the only source of light that was readily available when the electricity was cut off (which happened often), but they were nevertheless sincerely appreciated, for I always craved knowledge. Education is a journey to quench the craving that drives us to discover our existence, our purpose, and our contribution to the society we are placed in to excel.

My journey has been immensely transforming, so I am much indebted and grateful to Boston College in Lincolnshire in the United Kingdom for their trust in my ability to develop despite starting with a noticeable gap in knowledge. I am most indebted to Nottingham Trent University, also in the United Kingdom, for supporting me and providing me with the relevant lecturers, teaching materials, study materials, and direction in my career growth. At times it is indeed difficult to put up with those whose ambitions are bigger than their circumstances. My merit was judged constantly during the first few years of my European encounter as I adapted to the new academic world I had been placed in to compete. For this reason, I am indebted.

I would like to thank my parents, family, readers, supporters, and friends who have had to put up with my relentless and energetic outlook on life. Thanks also go to the wonderful government of the United Kingdom, which has made it possible for me to conclude my Masters through the provisions of its Student Loans Company. SLC enabled me to pursue my desired course without fear of not being able to afford it.

Special thanks goes to Kathie Moore, the dean of the School of Social Sciences at Nottingham Trent University, and Professor Edward Peck, vice-chancellor of Nottingham Trent University. Your leadership presences are impeccable.

Also, special thanks goes to my university tutor, James Stiller, for his outstanding assistance. James, you have always made the time to help me navigate any academic issue I might have at any given time throughout my masters. You also told me to ensure that I write in my own voice. From here forth, I will never stop writing. I have found my voice. I have found my passion, and I have found my sense of contribution: to help student believe in getting through any challenges academically, economically, and personally.

A final thanks goes to Jerry Nicholls and all his associates, for without him I wouldn't have had the opportunity to know that education and training are not exclusively confined and limited to academia but extend to the worlds outside it (personal, social, economic, and general business). Without them, I wouldn't be the senior manager I am today. Without them, I wouldn't know what it means to reach above and beyond with a brain, a heart, rolled-up sleeves, and two working hands.

This book is undoubtedly a contribution to all students at all levels, for it explains the significance of exams and education through a mind that has travelled to different worlds and fought against various common academic challenges like a soldier and conquered them triumphantly with everyone's support. Thank you!

A Gift

Education is a systematic gift—a gift from experience and a gift to experience. We as students must forward it on likewise in our various capacities, but not just the same as it was given to us. We must constantly engage with it, ponder it, analyse it, improve it, redesign it, and lastly, distribute it. To satisfy this implied obligation, we must apply our own originality and individuality and improve on them consistently. We must better ourselves through the constant search for exceptionality in knowledge, so when we are required to give education forward, we can give it better and give more of it to the very best of our acquisition.

—MSc Samson Yung-Abu

Author's Note

*Visualisation is a powerful tool of foresight when we embark
on a given objective because it gives the goal a special kind of
aroma that makes the hunger to finish it more constant and
bearable and the waiting more meaningful and magical.*

A piece of quick advice before you engage with this book fully: by the
end of this book, you should have a vivid idea of where you want to be at
the end of the year. The fact is, exams are an unavoidable part of being a
student. Some students have difficulty obtaining higher grades not because
they haven't worked hard enough in their studies but because there is a gap
in their understanding, approach, competence, and consistency when it
comes to preparing themselves for exams.

While hard work and perseverance are required during the academic
process, students who are familiar with exams understand that the exam
period is filled with all manner of unexpected events. These can be
anticipated, managed, and overcome if key elements are taken into account
and certain preliminaries explored. It is, however, rather difficult to predict
or minimise these risks without understanding why they happen and how
to approach them better. For this reason, I felt it was imperative that I write
this book.

Disheartened and discouraged, I got to a stage where just passing wasn't
enough. I wanted to do better and also achieve consistent top grades. Today,
for me, academic pressures are finally and officially over, as I hold my
master's degree in my hands, all credits neatly addressed and summarised
on size A4 paper with a sophisticated signature, ready to claim my place in

the world of modern professions. Better learning, after all, should lead to better earning.

Before you continue to turn the pages of this book, consider this analogy: Imagine for a moment how well you have to prepare for a flight to a specific destination—in particular, if you are going solo. What sort of thoughts and arrangements would you have to concern yourself with? Your mind will fill with thoughts like, *Where am I going? Do I have the right credentials to fly there (passport, ID, travel documents, visas)? When is my flight? Have I scheduled enough time to get to the airport? Where and how is it best to check in? What is the maximum luggage allowance? Am I carrying too much or too little? Do I need immunisations? What about money? Toiletries? Prescriptions? Meals? Accommodations?*

A similar thought pattern can form before exam periods: *When is the exam? What is the time, date, location? What subject area? How many questions? Have we covered it in class? How many hours should I study for? Do I have all the relevant information I need to study? Am I ahead with my revision? Do I need to cover more? What do I need to bring along during the exam? What am I permitted to use during the exam? Is it an open paper or a closed paper or an oral exam?*

Students who have failed to cover the questions proposed above are more likely to struggle to pass. They often find themselves failing miserably in exams even before the day comes, but why? The same principles apply to your pre-exam prep as your preflight prep, which will become clear as you read along. Without the proper assessment of what is needed, and without asking the right questions and answering them by taking the relevant and necessary actions, students can find themselves unprepared and taken by surprise by exam questions.

My Finest Hour

When we want something bad enough, we will do what is needed to get it. Intelligence can only go so far. Other things contribute to reaching the finish line successfully. These include in-depth research on the subject area, the right motivation, the necessary commitment, an ambitious mindset, a determined character, good study habits, and excellent writing skills.

While the academic year is long, winding, and sometimes like a rollercoaster, finally finishing a degree always feels good. It is the beginning of a new chapter in your life. The adventure continues, and you can now go on and do all the beautiful things you've only ever dared to dream of. All academic challenges previously faced are now behind you. In front of you is your degree in its physical form, with many prospects attached to it.

Holding the degree in your hand, you take a very deep breath, intrigued, and savour the unbelievable and incredible sight. You finally feel more employable, more mobile, more confident, more adaptable, and more convinced of what you are capable of. Your status has now been updated. Your capacity has been extended along with your level of intelligence. You are now more valuable. You twinkle.

With your degree in hand, you finally feel a profound sense of belief, of relief. All the turbulence during the long exam flight (the study period leading to it) has come to an end. You didn't crash; you arrived, you landed, and now you've claimed your luggage (your intended degree) successfully.

This is the power of the exam. It is like an automobile designed to drive you to your intended destination—from point A to point B, from school to college, from college to university, and so on—but only if you know the route, plan the route, and choose to follow the map (your *Student Exam Passport*).

Visualising Graduation

Starting with the end in mind is vital. Graduation is equivalent to a finish line. It remains the primary objective when a student makes a decision to apply for an academic or vocational course. Graduating is vital for each student because, once you have done it successfully, you can go on and do something more promising. Graduating the year with your peers is where you want to be at the end of that academic stage. It is deflating to not quite finish alongside your classmates, your academic journey companions. It is defeating to have to redo the year again, missing out on the graduation that you were supposed to be part of, and missing out on the stage you were supposed to transition into.

I come across students from time to time who have wasted the year and failed. They bear an exasperated expression when their peers are graduating and posting their achievements online, celebrating with big smiles and joyful tears. They start whispering to themselves, "I should be graduating today with them. I wish I had studied and not left it till the last minute."

Graduating is a massive accomplishment, the end before the beginning of another journey. While the exam period and graduation seem far from each other, students hold the connection in their hands. It is a beautiful moment to be part of the formal atmosphere, the incredible and colourful scenery, the graduation outfit, the cap, the gown, the proud parents all around you, the talented lecturers, the crowd, the lights, the entrance music, the cameras, the goosebumps, the speeches, the formal handshakes, and finally the congratulations onstage.

In hindsight, I realise that graduating is not just about the degree we acquire but about the person we become, the people we encounter, and the path we cross. It is about the fear we faced and the pace at which we grew; the dos we ignored and the don'ts we tried; the content we produced and the content we extended. It is about the million other things we had to do: the sacrifices, the junk food, the workload, the weight gain, the weight loss, the all-nighters, the insomnia, the bloodshot eyes, the headache, the emotional wreck, the dyslexia discovery, the adventure, the fun, the pressure, the team projects, the friends, the piggy-backing (relying on others to finish your work), the life partners, the housemates, the craves, the procrastination, the memes, the sesh. Yes, the sesh.

Our finest hour is getting through it all and having something tangible to show for it (the degree) and something intangible (the exceptional experience and personal growth). But among all, I realised that the best trophies one could acquire in life are the knowledge, friendship, and overall expertise obtained during the process of achievement in life.

I hope you chose to take the chance now and learn all the beautiful things this book can offer that would make your academic life proceed in competence and confidence, and in so doing prepare you better for all your exams. At the end of this book, you as a student will have no reason to doubt your capacity to learn better and achieve the best grades you can have. All the accessories for taking an exam are in here. Dive in!

Exam Quotes

- Get inspired and motivated before you get started, so you don't get all worked up and give up.
- At some point, you have to start revising to pass your upcoming exams. You will have to start somewhere. Right now is available.
- It is not easy to pass exams, but it is simple. Prioritise, prepare, and put studying ahead of everything else.
- Some students call it pressure, some call it push—whatever you think it is, make it your drive to succeed.
- You can't delegate good grades. You have got to put in the work.
- If you put the work in, you will get the worth out.

Chapter 1

Foresight

The closest we can get to knowing the outcome of something before it happens is through available examples of experience that occur in hindsight. This chapter introduces students to a visual preliminary to an exam, with the primary purpose of foresight into planning and anticipation.

I recollect in my early stages of academic learning how unprepared I was, how predictable my poor performance was, and how it impacted my ability to predict certain academic failure. I struggled to write exceptional examination essays. I failed to recall specific dates, names, key facts, theories, definitions, and formulas. How frustrating and agonising it felt! Unsatisfied, I started looking into ways to predict better, anticipate better, and prepare better for better academic performance and results.

Preliminary

In hindsight, the majority of exam failure could have been predicted, managed, and overcome. The failing memory when you forget relevant facts, the surprise questions you didn't expect, the nervousness before the exam, the anxiety during the exam, the breakdown after the exam, and the inevitable fail on result day—all of these could have been prevented.

In this chapter, you'll have the advantage of imagining what happens due to lack of planning and anticipation and discovering how best to prevent it by avoiding a scenario similar to one that follows. It is vital that students have a vivid picture and understanding of possible outcomes or consequences based on how they choose to approach exams. This knowledge can lead their exam preparation to better specific actions before exam day. To understand the consequences of anything, we usually need a rough idea of how it is likely to end. This is where experience becomes the best teacher.

The Scenario

Imagine this: Rather than spend the revision period studying and revising effectively, you didn't. Instead, you spent the months leading up to the exam watching soap operas and YouTube videos, procrastinating on social media, and doing other everyday activities that students usually do to avoid sitting down and studying.

Imagine that exam day finally arrives as scheduled, and you are sitting in your designated seat, knees under the table, backpack and other belongings out of reach. You are vaguely calm. Imagine listening to the instructor passing all manner of instructions and directions in great torrents: *Do, don't, should, shouldn't, touch, don't touch. Ignore everyone and everything except that question paper in front of you. But for now, just stare at it. Don't touch; don't turn over. Just don't!* You are vaguely and half-heartedly paying attention to all that information because you are scared, anxious, almost giddy, and eager to get on and over with the exam.

Imagine that the exam paper sits neatly in front of you, static, a nice, non-transparent, A4-sized paper. But you can't see what's on the other side before you are permitted to. Your hands are sweaty. Your heart is pounding, racing, almost rattling inside you. But all you can do is stare at the blank back of the question paper—curiously, nervously eager to see what's on the other side.

Then, suddenly, you get the go-ahead: "You can now begin." Students turn the paper over quicker than lightning, including you. Your eyes dart over the questions looking for a familiar word, but none is found. It instantly becomes apparent that you haven't covered the questions now in front of you. Your preparation was vague, diluted, and in all honesty, painfully insufficient. Clutching your pen, you realise your ill-preparedness. The clues were ignored. Study techniques were omitted or poorly acknowledged.

In awful silence, you try harder to recollect. Distraught and desperate for recollection, your memory begins to fail you. The facts can't come forward; they can't be retrieved. But why? As this book will reveal, you haven't assumed sufficient accountability prior to the exam. You've failed to understand the fundamental elements of effective memory techniques and application. When the pressure is on and the time is ticking, your heart beats heavier, quicker, abnormally. Your brain is frozen and unresponsive. Time is now of the essence. Pressure and time don't play too well in our favour as humans.

The next five minutes feel like an hour. You see your day begin to end. You swallow hard as everything rapidly crashes down on you, and you feel agitated, confused, and nervous. You're ready to cave in. *Hand in the towel*, your brain almost pleads. After another failed attempt to retrieve information that is simply not there, you consult the clock behind the instructor standing in front of the students, alert, solemn-faced, vigilantly watching every itch, twitch, and general movement in the room. Ten more minutes quickly pass.

You decide to try again—to have another go. You go through the unchanged questions again, hoping for a sign, a signal, familiarity, something comforting. You seek a question you can identify with—one that, with a stroke of luck, you can pass with. You try to recollect and fail, so you try harder. You realise you are stuck. You realise that in the last twenty minutes, you only prolonged the inevitable. Inside, you cry, defeated.

Twenty minutes into your struggle to pick and answer the questions, you manage to look around. The guy ahead of you is deep in writing. He looks calm, alert, all clued in. He seems prepared and assured; he flows. The girl on your right seems to be reflecting the guy's pace. The guy on your left hasn't stopped writing since the instructor said you could start. At that point, you finally realise you have let yourself down.

CHAPTER 2

Objectives

Objectives are always where we should start, for they give outcomes purpose, value, and genuine meaning. Setting an objective is a conscious act of pinpointing where your finish line should be and mapping all the places you shouldn't stop at.

The previous chapter presented an essential element in the process of taking exams. Students who are not aware of how badly lack of preparation can impact on the overall experience and outcome of their academic achievements end up failing because they cannot predict common errors by poor-performing students. In this sense, the first objective is to be adequately prepared from the outset. The number-one aim of this book is to facilitate the above student objective.

Some institutions find it difficult to keep individual students fully engaged in their academic affairs. There are many books and guides that provide tips on how to successfully take oral, written, and practical exams; write research papers; read articles; write dissertations; complete projects; and so on. With such revision guides at their disposal, why can't students achieve better grades? Why can't they finish the academic year with fireworks in their eyes and satisfaction in their achievements?

This book is not in any way intended as a substitute for study guides; it complements them. It aims to support students in their exam preparation, facilitate mobility, and provide mental clarity. Most important, it enables students to go through their exam preparation at a pace that does not require a lot of time, considering other practical study guides and study materials they might have to go through.

To achieve its objective, this book provides students with imperative, comprehensive, and informative explanations, instructions, and guidelines on how to take an exam with the right awareness, competence, state of mind, calmness, and boldness. Various chapters outline topics such as the aim of an exam, the significance of memory, the essence of forgetting, and the value of accountability. The book is brief and concise, but it includes all the relevant tools you might need to engage with your study material or study guides. It proposes a more fundamental way of thinking about your role in the academic period leading up to and after your exam.

Awareness in planning can help you anticipate potential barriers to learning and improve understanding of and engagement with revision materials, which can minimise stress and increase confidence before a significant assessment or a major exam. (All exams should be treated as major; it builds a disciplined character.) As indicated previously, much of this book expands on a student's need for personal accountability, preparation, and organisation before exams. These concepts are crucial to becoming a high-performing student.

One reason many students fail is that revision guides are too rigid and lengthy. Students who struggle with time management need all the time they can get and are in desperate need of help, guidance, and more time. We can all accept that students have real-world problems that interfere with their work in the academic world, and some of these problems are unavoidable. They include jobs, family issues, social issues, and even health issues. There are also individual differences in learning styles and understanding. Some study guides overlook this aspect, and students don't know how to adapt the provided techniques.

Chapter 3

Elements of Competence

Competence is the backbone of performance.
Lack of competence produces a limp result.

For students, it is perhaps the dominant view that whether they pass or fail depends primarily on the teacher or academic institution. While students should expect their teachers and institutions to be competent in preparing them for exams, the same is required of all students at some point, particularly during exams. This chapter focuses on shifting academic responsibility away from teachers and institutions and towards students.

While the responsibility is somewhat upon teachers to adequately prepare students for any examination, there is a limit to how far they can or should facilitate this obligation. A competent teacher understands that from the beginning of the semester, students should be directed to carry out independent learning. This is because teachers know from experience that assigning responsibility to students promotes self-confidence in independent learning and gives a sense of control over the capacity to acquire more knowledge independently.

While individual students in the same academic institution or similar ones consistently benefit from better grades on exams, some students are not adequately informed from the outset about certain prerequisites. I remember a couple of years back, a classmate was furious about failing an exam. With exasperation, he said that the teacher was stupid, the college was useless, and the whole educational system was a mess and a waste of his time because it didn't prepare him for the exam.

After listening with eyebrows raised, I replied, "Hold on. We go to the same school. We have the same classes. We took the same exam. How come I passed if the teacher was stupid, the college was useless, and the institution was a flat mess?"

He shrugged, went silent, and said nothing—which usually means *I agree. I just wanted a good moan.*

If, when placed in the same environment and given the same competent teacher and the same time to study and revise before exams, some students achieve excellence and others diminish in their academic achievement, there must be factors outside the control of the teacher. These can include poor reading habits, poor study habits, poor revision technique, lack of time management, inability to filter out relevant information, lack of motivation, poor emotional balance, lack of independent learning, and personal issues. It should follow that students who perform exceptionally and gain top grades in their various exams show a level of exceptionality that can only be the result of exercising personal academic responsibility in and after class hours through independent learning.

Exceptionality does not come by students doing their academic work in a mundane manner, or by giving mundane effort in the classroom and blaming it on their teachers. It does not come by closing the textbook once the school day closes and failing to do the required homework or failing to read through the required reading list. It does not happen by choosing TV over homework when you get back home. It comes by going through the lessons outside the classroom, prioritising homework over homies, and doing out-of-class homework promptly. It comes by taking each daily teaching from the classroom further into your spectrum, expanding it, and then going above and beyond with it before exam time comes.

One of the major mistakes students make is waiting for the exam period to commence before they begin to work through their textbooks, notes, and other study and revision materials. Evidence of this is always visible in their final piece of academic work. Most students who fail to achieve a good grade have failed to notice that examiners are somewhat aware of what top-grade work should consist of. Examiners do this year in and year out. They have a developed mental and physical cross-check list to tick when they mark individual work. To this end, an exceptional piece of work always showcases something distinctive—something that indicates that the student has taken the overall semester teaching up a notch or two. The student has gone above and beyond with their independent learning.

Now that you know the basic principles and your role in the learning process, it is time to understand the initial expectation during the actual exam: proof of academic competence. Students should know that examiners are looking for something persuasive in content, and they can only award you with marks that befit your work. Your finished examination paper is what tells the examiner that you have attained the necessary knowledge to construct a persuasive piece of academic work. Such work should demonstrate an ability to answer, identify, explain, introduce, incorporate, discuss, structure, argue, analyse, and evaluate any given question promptly and a coherent expression.

Over the years I have come across students who are uninterested, unmotivated, or uninformed throughout an academic period. They end up failing as a consequence of their disengagement with the academic year. Their work during markings usually lacked persuasion. It often lacked the above-stated components.

Early exposure to the expectations of the burden of proof of academic competence as mentioned above could facilitate better engagement with these students' academic affair. Students who strive during the exam are those who undertake independent learning outside the classroom. For instance, students are given a specific reading list to go through during certain periods in the semester. This represents a shift in responsibility. When students go on and do those readings, they automatically have an advantage over students who do not.

Even though there are tons of guides out there on exam revision—a truckload—some students still manage to do poorly. They fail, and in extreme situations fully log out, whereby they delete education completely. They hand in the towel. They give up. They quit. And then, they regret it later on in life. One reason for this is that they haven't done enough outside-the-class learning. They haven't carried out any independent learning or perhaps have done some in a mundane and purposeless manner. Some revision books fail to emphasise the need for accountability in a way that enables a student to understand that the outcome of their exam is to a considerable extent personally controllable. It is mostly dependent on how they choose to approach the period leading up to the exam.

Over the years, I have realised that there is only so much a teacher can do to help a student. For instance, in a recent one-on-one lesson, one of my students explained to me that he had a mock exam, and he didn't pass it.

"How many hours have you studied this week?" I asked.

He shrugged, then instantly his eyes met his shoes. After a moment of silence, he lifted his head back up to me with an embarrassed gaze. After another minute of silence, he blurted something to the effect that he hadn't done any studies. We were now heading into the end of the week—it was Friday night—and he hadn't done any out-of-class reading or studying.

"So, you mean that all week, you have not touched your books after class?" I asked.

"No," he replied.

"Listen," I said calmly, "you should always spend at least ten or twelve hours each week going through all you have learned during your classes—revising and making notes to address, to inquire about, to ponder on. Furthermore, these hours should exclude the hours you spend on your homework."

After he took it all in, he nodded hurriedly and said, "That's true."

"You can't expect your teachers to do everything for you," I added. "They won't be sitting your exams for you, and they certainly won't be having their names on your results, you know," I added.

He nodded, again. He got the picture that he needed to take more responsibility for his own good before he was required to account for it at any given time, perhaps during a random mock exam or an actual exam—a decisive one!

Expanding the Proof of Academic Competence

Throughout each academic semester, teachers are expected, to the best of their ability, to educate students as outlined in the academic syllabus to a common gold standard provided by the governing academic institution and prepare each student for upcoming exams. This is a teacher's duty, responsibility, job, and primary purpose. However, this expectation shifts during the period leading to the actual assessments, in which students are expressly or implicitly required to show how much they have learned and how much they have improved intellectually and competently. At this stage, the academic responsibility shifts to the student and becomes a proof of academic competence. The institution says, "Prove to us that you have what it takes to move up to the next stage in the academic ladder."

Competence in this sense can be described as the ability to excel when placed in a particular position or in a specific situation (mock or real exam) at any given time. Conclusively, students are expected to show competence in performance and deliver exceptional results based on the content they covered during the period of teaching and lecturing. Students who showcase proficiency at this stage during the semester are the ones who satisfy the examiners that they merit the transition.

Chapter 4

Why Exams?

While education might be the door to success, exams are the key to that door.

The previous chapters have covered some basics of the nature of exams, their impact, possible outcomes, and individual responsibilities. This chapter is where we really come to terms with the essence of the exam: what is it for, and more importantly, why do we do it?

As students, nothing, and I mean *nothing*, worries us more than a decisive exam, one that lasts a few hours but could determine the course of our academic, social, and personal life. Individually, we each have specific things that worry us—like money, family matters, future career, illnesses, and mental health—but collectively, the familiar concept that concerns us all, even if just for a brief period, is exams.

Exams are often required to attain certain credentials; obtain sufficient grades to transit into the next academic stage; get into the school, college, or university of our choice; or even get the job we want. While exams are not conclusive determinants of our future as students, they are at times relevant, inevitable, unavoidable, and necessary to get into other areas, both academic and personal. Due to their essential nature, they are always going to be around to test our ability to move up to the next stage in our academic and personal life.

Exams can, therefore, be one of the most crucial determinants in how we proceed in life, in particular for students who have set an expectation for themselves, such as a dream job, or have had one set for them by their families. Some students are not sure why they even have to take exams. Some assume exams are a means of torture or punishment, a barrier, or an irrelevant and time-wasting activity.

In fact, exams are merely tools to assess your ability to be prepared, be organised, contribute, take responsibility, accept accountability, and perform exceptionally and competently. Students who go through an exam or a test are able to see how they are doing in class. Teachers are able to monitor students' progress, while the institution is able to monitor the progress of both teachers and students.

An exam is an act of analysis aimed at a specific target (humans/ animals/technology) with the intention of ascertaining the level at which individuals currently operate or identifying the physical fitness level they now occupy, for purposes of comparison or adjustment. It is simply a measuring instrument. Academically speaking, the primary purpose of an exam is to establish a student's level of intellectual knowledge in relation to the teaching materials that the student has been exposed to. Exams are a platform on which each student can transition from one academic stage to the next in a way that showcases excellence and high performance. This is not just on a national scale but is the consensus worldwide.

Nevertheless, I often hear students whisper in complaint and frustration, "Are exams even necessary?"

"Are exams really needed in real life?"

"What is the point, if we can't use algebra, Pythagoras, circumference, or pie charts in real life?"

"Who needs a medical qualification if you can just google the symptoms and get instant answers?"

It should be advised that this are misleading thoughts and dangerous at best.

I have even heard student making statements such as, "Education is a waste of time, because exams are unnecessary and inapplicable in real life situation."

Students begin to develop a conflicting sense of, "Are exams really worth the effort?"

"They might be right."

"I might be wasting my time studying for this exam when I can't do anything with it."

"Are they right in what they are saying?"

"Should I give up now?"

Key advice is to stay away from such a thought process, in particular during your revision period. Don't be misled by the dogma that education is not a guarantee of success. That logic expresses a level of ignorance and mediocracy that only the unsuccessful would ascribe to. Never forget that mediocracy is a category, a little tiny box, a tiny birdcage, founded on doubt and built by the very same people who now inhabit it. Qualifications derived from education through exams are indicators of a deeper level of competence in a specific field.

One day when this debate came up, I had the opportunity to enlighten another student. He said, "Doctors are stupid. They just have the qualification and think that they can tell me what to do. Like, I can google that stuff online."

I remembered him going to the dentist when he was in agonising pain, whimpering, suffering, and unable to sleep or study. I reminded him of that. "Why did you go to the dentist last month, Patrick?"

"The painkiller didn't stop the pain," he answered with a smart shrug.

I said, "Why didn't you go to a mechanic or a plumber or your next-door neighbour? Or Larry, the student upstairs?"

He went silent. He knew what I was getting at.

I charged on. "It is simply because you trusted the dentist, because you knew he was accredited and had the skills and the qualification for the job, which can't be learned just by looking at online slides accumulated on Google or Wikipedia. If I told you he had no qualifications, would you have gone to him?" I enquired.

The student shook his head and whispered, "No." He got the point.

I said to him, "A qualification is derived from understanding certain technicalities that can only be taught in certain academic institutions by certain academic individuals who have also attained certain qualifications that suggest competence in that specific area. They are specialised professionals. You as a citizen deeply know this, and you trust them." A qualification gives citizens a sense of trust that they are in the right qualified hands and that the remedy they seek will be delivered with the utmost care, diligence, and professionalism.

With the technicalities of the modern world now, specific fields are growing at a fast pace that demands competence from individuals. For this reason, exams have become paramount in ensuring that individuals who decide to take up technical roles in these fields have shown proof of competence in that subject area. To this end, an exam is a powerful tool. Academically speaking, exams are about identifying the progress of proficiency, measuring competence, and rewarding excellence in achievements. Exams enable academic and career institutions to outline a student's academic strengths and weaknesses so an appropriate measure of help can be provided. Furthermore, an exam is a resilience builder. If adequately engaged with, an exam enables each student to build a progressive layered character for future career purposes.

One of the primary objectives of each educational institution should be to ensure that each student develops in parallel with the next student. Exam are, therefore, a critical element in the process of learning. They identify areas that need addressing or applauding. Students who are keen on progression are always looking forward to finding out how well they have done this time or how well they need to do next time.

It should be advised that exams are not just about measuring individual competition for knowledge or attaining enough credits on one's qualification. They are also about determining the level of competence a student has developed and what area a teacher should focus the most on. They are about placing responsibility on students so they are accountable for the result they want to produce. They are about showing students how to control the outcome they want and materialise it in an efficient, timely manner—a skill set also relevant in life outside of academia.

An exam is also a powerful tool when it comes to time management. Students who can showcase excellence in various exam subjects are considered to be more organised, capable of managing their time, resilient in the face of challenges, and able to work under pressure. All of these are vital elements in real-life situation, in real-life jobs, and in the general social environment. In a nutshell and in no hierarchical order, exams are necessary for:

- strengthening rational and critical thinking
- showing competence and composure in written work
- gauging strengths and weakness
- assessing how well an academic institution is doing
- providing a promising national economic and attracting international individuals
- pursuing career paths
- exhibiting comprehension when posed with difficulties
- demonstrating the relevance of preparation and research when competing for a desired job
- enhancing mental performance (priming the brain to be productive and creative with efficiency and richness in thinking)
- enhancing motor skills
- exposing students to responsibility and accountability
- preparing students for life outside academia

Universality of Exams

Exams as we know them are not just a national affair but a global phenomenon. It is not only a score on a piece of paper or computer but an illustration of measured competence in a tangible form recognized all around the world. Exams are the language of the globe, a tool that signifies similarity across different countries, a tangible consensus that can be used in various parts of the world to test competence in individual knowledge. It is, in essence, a universal assessment method for mental fitness.

Each country understands that exams save second-guessing and speculation as to what individual student or institutions can or can't do. Exams predict future grades and measure gaps in academic affairs. Conclusively, exam results speak on individuals' behalf and even on behalf of educational institutions. Exams declare our competence and potential.

Countries around the world value student competence as much as economic status in an attempt to attract top students and educators from around the globe. Every three years, the Organization for Economic Cooperation and Development tests 15-year-olds around the world (in seventy-two countries and economies) using a data-collection method called the Programme for International Student Assessment. It assesses students' math, science, and reading capabilities. At present, Singapore is ranked as the best in these areas in comparison to competing countries.

I came to the UK from Germany with a limited understanding of the language, the culture, and the academic process. Before that, I moved to Germany from Africa, with a similar set of circumstances. I knew not one word of German when I started high school. I sat in a class where a language was spoken which I knew nothing about. I couldn't even say "Good morning." Yet I passed high school and went on to pre-college and passed that, all through exams.

I wasn't prepared for any of it, but I knew I had no choice but to discover how to learn better, speak better, think better, perform better, and write in a more sophisticated way. Throughout this journey, I was a dedicated student, and I still am today. In retrospect, I found commonalities in all levels of student life: the cluttered study desk, the shortage of sleep, the exam pressure, the stress, the unpredictability in questions asked, the confusion, the panic, the worries, and most importantly, the sense of accountability that is a prerequisite to exam success.

To my academic knowledge, exams are not presented on what we have never been taught before; exams are set on what we have been through during a specific academic period (weeks, months, or years). Students are expected to have acquired the competence required to take an exam. The burden of proving competence is passed down to the individual student, a shift that involves accountability of further independent engagement with the study materials. This is crucial for all levels of education: preschool, primary school, secondary school, high school, and college, both undergraduate and graduate.

Exams are quite frightening because of the premise of difficulty in exam-taking, which is given more praise than it deserves. Overcoming exam struggles is cognitively essential as well as practical. Ask yourself: *What does taking this exam mean to me? Is it personal and in any way important to progress to my next life stage academically, personally, and socially?* Mentally analysing current study habits, planning, organisation, and anticipation before you sit down and revise is important. As the rest of this book will highlight, you ought to go over these details, declutter your mind, prepare, and then proceed with revising.

CHAPTER 5

Flight or Fail

Without departing, you will never arrive, and without adequate
preparation, departure will never occur. A successful arrival,
therefore, is where preparation has been accounted for at departure.

Taking an exam could be compared to a flight to any destination, as briefly explained at the beginning of this book. It is devastating to end up somewhere you don't want to be or didn't plan to go. We are less likely to go to a destination we have no interest in and haven't researched, and one we don't have the right credentials for. This is because if we do, the only thing that would welcome us is failure. Turbulence is okay—it's inevitable—and a little stress is also okay.

However, such stress should be unavoidable stress rather than avoidable stress. An avoidable pressure is one that is caused by fear of lack of preparation because you anticipate that you have not done all you can or should do to be adequately prepared. This is often a consequence of your actions or lack of actions. With this in mind, here are five concepts to consider before you begin to study:

1. accountability
2. learning style
3. preparation
4. priorities: time management

Accountability

As students, we consciously or subconsciously place a great deal of accountability on our teachers, lecturers, and tutors. We believe that it is their sole responsibility to help us pass our exams, and when we fail, we start pointing fingers and throwing blame around. Not long ago, I had a meeting with one of my lecturers at Trent University in Nottingham, who made that point. It got me thinking, and through this, I was inspired yet again to finish this book—and in particular, this chapter.

Accountability is not the primary responsibility of our teachers. It is a collective responsibility that at different stages shifts positions. Accountability is not an obligation but an effort by both your teacher and yourself as a student to reach the best possible results beneficial to both you (the student) and the teacher. In my first book, *My Student Pledge Journal*, I emphasised the need for keeping a journal, engaging better with your academic studies, and staying committed. All of these tips tie together with your responsibility to study efficiently. It's personal, it's specific, and it's all on you.

Our teachers, tutors, and lecturers are required to equip us with the relevant materials, explain as much as possible about the subjects and concepts we should know, and point us in the direction that we should read around. However, we are primarily responsible for consolidating, remembering, recalling, and extending our understanding of the materials we have been provided with before the assessment or exam.

I once took an exam during my A levels at Boston College in Lincolnshire. It was a three-hour business exam. I failed it the first time (U) and passed it the second time (A). There was no middle ground. Why? I held myself accountable, not my teachers. I realised that if I really wanted the grade bad enough, I would go out of my way to get it. I studied really hard and learned from my previous ill revision. I read the same materials but with a different mindset. I just couldn't afford to fail the same exam twice. I had my UCAS points to meet, and another failure would set me back and increase the workload. Plus, I wanted to enjoy the forecasted hot summer that was approaching with my friends.

I thought to myself, *If you can pass an exam the second time, you can surely pass it the first time.* This was now my accountability side-thinking. Furthermore, I thought about the consequences if I failed and what I would do differently if I were to pass it the second time. With these thoughts in mind, I worked hard, put the books first above everything else, and avoided any form of distraction.

Avoid means *avoid*. At one point, I said I would avoid social media, and I did … until I decided I would quickly check one message. Before I knew it, I was clicking, browsing, liking, and uploading. It happened, a lot, and after a while I realised my limitations, so now I avoid social media totally when revising. I place my phone far away from my designated study area and primarily focus on the revision as scheduled.

Learning Style

Before you engage with any study materials, it is vital to understand how you learn. Knowing your learning style makes things much easier. Efficiency is paramount; it's a key component of learning and remembering. We tend to remember better when we learn in a way that feels easy.

Education is not easy, as any student will tell you. However, it becomes easier for some students because they have developed a way of learning that is unique and personal to them. Over the years, we all have heard people say things like:

> "I learn better this way."
> "I like to read the textbook, highlight the notes, and go over them."
> "I learn better during the day."
> "I learn better at night."
> "I learn better when I can see things done in front of me."
> "I learn better in a quiet place alone."
> "I learn better around friends."
> "I learn better when I listen to what I have to learn"

All of these learning habits are specific and personal to those individuals. So now the question is, what is *your* learning style? Below are several learning styles. Reflecting on which one best describes your own way of learning could put you in a much better position when revising.

- **Visual:** You feel more comfortable and remember more using pictures, images, and spatial mind maps during learning.
- **Aural:** You feel more comfortable using sound and music for learning.
- **Verbal:** You feel more comfortable and remember more using words, both in speech and writing during learning.
- **Kinaesthetic:** You feel more comfortable and remember more using your body, hands, and sense of touch during learning.

Preparation

Now that we have identified our role in the exam process, we can proceed to establish the value of preparation and planning. Some students go into the exam period without any prior planning, which inevitably exposes them to unanticipated barriers that lead to poor exam performance. Preparation, as we know, is not a new concept for any student when it comes to exams. We all know it is a critical aspect of the pre-exam period. Some students still manage to forget the whole preparation period until the last minute, when anxiety and stress come out to play with their minds.

Some students are notorious for this kind of last-minute preparation. Preparation requires a considerable amount of energy, planning, time, and purpose if we want to perform better in exams; it is unavoidable. Preparation is the shortest route to getting ahead, staying ahead, and finishing ahead. By taking the time to reflect on and analyse our current reading habits, revision habits, and free-time habits—and figure out how best to adjust and implement them—we will improve our academic performance. This is where preparation comes in. Preparation is what makes the exam journey smoother, less stressful, more manageable, and more meaningful.

Some students find out late when the exam dates are, what the questions are likely to be, what they should have focused on, etc. They haven't done adequate research, asked the right questions, and managed their time well. All of this could lead to failure in exams. Students who exhibit these habits tend to fail because of lack of adequate preparation and planning. They open the exam paper, and all they can see is: *Question 1: unfamiliar. Question 2: frightening. Question 3: failure. Question 4: I am doomed. Question 5: I give up.* Avoiding the element of surprise is essential.

While pressure could be a motivator to more effective revision, last-minute study and preparation is a poor habit and a risky way to approach necessary and decisive exams. There are, of course, articles on how to revise in one day and so on, but students who adhere to such practices will learn that there is a limit to how far they can get. At some point, they will be caught out, and it could be during a final exam. My advice would be to refrain from last-minute studying, prepare as early as you can afford to, and put study ahead of less immediate responsibilities.

According to Benjamin Franklin, when we fail to prepare, we are inevitably preparing to fail. This signifies and places the art of preparation as a foundation for success. How you prepare—the when, where, and why—is very important. Before you physically prepare, it is important to be mentally prepared. Start by thinking about what you want out of the pending exam. Do you want to pass or fail? Why do you want to pass? Do you have to pass? All these questions are important. While they sound basic and common-sense, they are nevertheless not considered by some students.

To give more meaning to something we want to achieve, we need the reasons to be personal and specific. One reason I started working harder during my college exams were that I wanted to move on to the next academic stage (UCAS points; degree; career; and making myself and my family proud). I knew from previous experience that failing only added more pressure and took up time that could be better utilised in other areas of my studies and social life.

It is important to gather up relevant textbooks and other practical study tools, such as previous academic notes, Post-it notes, highlighters, flash cards, study guides, and anything else you may consider helpful to enhance your revision. Avoid beginning a study session without the proper supplies or relevant information you should be focusing on. If unsure, consult with your teacher/lecturer, institution, or friends. Someone will have valid, useful advice for you.

Priorities: Time Management

As students, at times we are overwhelmed by activities, some unimportant and some critical. While the unimportant ones could be easily put aside with sufficient effort, other events are harder to set aside. The latter are most likely the ones most students struggle with, and this is where they have to work on prioritisation. There are undoubtedly individual circumstances which give prioritising a different meaning and structure. However, students should carefully consider what is on their to-do list and make a plan for how to make it through without compromising their studies and exam preparation.

Rather than starting your day by making a plan or setting an objective, plan your day and objectives the day before with a definite end to each. What do I mean by a definite end? Have something at the end of a plan—deadlines or a specific date—rather than vagueness. Priorities are better determined if we can identify the deadline tags attached to them. Once we have identified the ones with deadline tags, we can put them on a priorities list in such a way that the early deadlines get sorted out before the later deadlines. To perform this task efficiently, it is encouraging to have and maintain a record of all your priorities. At the end of this book, a schedule box "Revision Organiser Table" has been designed for this specific purpose.

CHAPTER 6

Top Grades: Starting with the End in Mind

Top grade is like a skyscraper. It takes an effort to get to the top, but once you are there, it feels like heaven. You feel a deeper sense of accomplishment—a gratifying achievement.

This chapter is one of the crucial chapters in this book. It aims to provide students and readers with a broad perspective on how to achieve a consistent top grade in an exam. Top grade, in essence, is every student's secret academic wish.

Generally, students who attain top grades such as As, Bs, first-class, or second-class are not just intelligent or naturally born smart. They are hard-working, and they acknowledge and implement specific study routines. The common presumption is that "The study period is really stressful, so if I can just get a pass mark, I will be glad." Such thoughts take away the element of aiming higher and working efficiently to achieve such an aim. They restrict students' opportunity to perform at their very best. Students who intend to achieve top marks in any exam should start with the end in sight. Aim for a top grade even before you begin planning your revision and study schedule.

Students who aim to pass often miss the opportunity to reach the minimum pass mark or, worse scenario, fail badly. In comparison, even on their worst day, students who aim for top marks never fail to reach the minimum pass mark. By the end of this chapter, readers should have gained an advanced understanding and insight on what top grades mean, their relevance for present and future purposes, and how students can attain them.

For most students, the exam is not over until the final result (the pass/ fail, the letter grading style, or the plus/minus grading system) is known. After each exam, we continue to stress in various degrees. We wait. We reflect. We worry. We sweat it. We attempt to predict our grades. We become uncertain that we have done all we could do. A logical reason for this is that our end result is usually a reflection of our exam preparation, which would show in our exam performance leading to our end result. It follows that grade equals performance and performance equals preparation (preparation = performance = grade). By understanding certain fundamentals in relation to achieving a top grade on exams, we stand a better chance of anticipating, predicting, and equipping ourselves for our exam.

Why Is Achieving Top Grades Important?

Top grades and exam success are about understanding the role you play as a student right from the onset to the day you sit the exam. They are about understanding the art of how you learn to learn and understanding how to apply that to what you have to learn. Top grades are essential to both your education institution and outside academia.

Examiners are really looking for distinction during their markings. They are all too used to seeing the same piece of writing, structure, etc. They want to see a deeper level of understanding in a piece of work that demonstrates beyond mere explanation to an application of supplementary key knowledge and uniqueness. Top grades are relevant to demonstrate competence in knowledge and application in exams and similar assessments and to ensure that students have the required skills to transition from academic life to career life.

In a competitive modern era like today, individuals who demonstrate top grades in their academic period are more likely to draw attention in a competitive market where academic qualification is required for specific jobs. This is particularly so because top grades showcase characteristics that go beyond intelligence, such as the capacity to perform under time pressure, be adequately prepared, and be organised. Students who accomplish top grades are able to displays their history (CV) in a fashion that reveals not just high standards in performance but consistency and growth.

While top grades are not a guarantee of success and acceptance, they put you in a different spotlight from other competitors. It is easier to distinguish yourself from other top-grade candidates when you have top grades. They give you more merit and justification as to why you should be considered for the job.

Trait or Skill?

Is the ability to get top grades a trait or a skill? I contend it is a skill that can be acquired, similar to writing and analysing skills in essays. As such, it should be invested in. Readers who wish to develop this skill set should bear in mind that it relies on consistency in focus and fluidity in adaptation through feedback, setbacks, and hard work. Students should be ready to explore a wide variety of written materials and synthesise these with their current level of knowledge. It is not an easy skill to master, but with sufficient practice, you can get the hang of it.

Arriving at a top grade in an exam involves a build-up of hard work, determination to succeed, and effective independent revision. But it doesn't stop there. It expands into applying that build-up in a way that demonstrates competence in application of key concepts and displays clarity in understanding, coherence, and a succinct flow. Remember, most examiners mark papers following a guideline. Guidelines are objectively constructed and leave little room for the subjective opinion of the examiners. By demonstrating a build-up and showing competence in understanding and application, you are heading for a top grade.

In most professions or career paths, top grade is a prerequisite, and even in cases where it is not expressly stated, it should be assumed to be the case. This is because, post-academia, individuals are often required to produce work that matches the quality of a top-grader. A top-grade piece of work displays high quality of material, sufficient research and preparation, analysis, and application. In a world full of young and competitive candidates, distinction in prior achievement seems to be one of the best predictors of acceptance when it comes to a job application.

Getting a top grade in an exam is not just about hard work or writing out a lengthy essay. It involves going beyond mere explanation of a topic or concept to the skilful application of key facts in a way that showcases extensive knowledge that is unambiguous, transparent, and well thought of. How do you achieve this level of expression? By engaging in more in-depth reading, understanding the basics of what you have to learn, and applying the relevant key facts (dates, names, concepts, formulas, etc) in coherent, structured, and relevant essay style.

Difficulty in achieving top grades despite hard work can be explained by two dilemmas: ineffective use of information and lack of sufficient research. To attain top grades, students should focus on the main topics in the syllabus and plan with any information they might have gathered through their syllabus and their teacher/lecturer. Students who perform best in their examinations are distinguishable by how well they have planned and the content of their write-up on their exam papers during marking.

To attain top grades, distinguish between essential and non-important facts before beginning the process of note-taking for exam studies. Avoid highlighting a colossal amount of information in your textbooks; it only leads to a temptation to want to know everything, even information you are not required to understand. The information you take in is of paramount importance.

Quality Matters When Information Is Involved

As students, we are consumers of information. We crave information. We seek it. We study it, consolidate it, understand it, recreate it, expand it, put it to memory, recollect it, and then use it to our advantage in required situations.

Think of information as a product for a minute. As with any product, we have to know how to use it, perhaps for health and safety reasons or simply to get our money's worth. As with any product we might come across, if not used in the right way, it becomes ineffective and a waste of time and money. We are required to understand how to use a product before we use it. We are required to understand the information written on the prescription side before we take it. Failure to follow instructions could be detrimental and lead to severe consequences. It follows that, when it comes to information, understanding is better than assumption or memorising.

Students who rely heavily on assumptions of what a piece of information is for or who memorise information just for recollection purposes have failed to understand the specification of that information. This is because every piece of information is available for a specific reason and should not simply be taken at face value. Examiners often see this in submitted exam papers. A memorised answer sheet lacks a deeper level of a coherent knowledge and application.

Memorisation is like drag-and-drop. It restricts the integration of relevant information in a purposeful and valuable way, and it does not allow for structure and succinctness. In addition, apart from understanding information for the benefit of general care and safety, understanding information for academic purposes is a better step toward winning top marks and achieving exceptional results.

The key is to digest the information you have accumulated in a time-efficient manner. Some students achieve this through mind mapping, fact isolation, drawing, or simply taking relevant selective notes. To achieve top grades, students would need to be able to extract important information from voluminous amounts of information. They should be willing to practice the art of extracting relevant important data from different required sources. There are books available on better writing, critical reading, evaluating, and reflective thinking. Students are therefore able to do some research in this area.

Another relevant point during an exam is to be able to produce a well-structured essay. An exam essay says a lot about how prepared a student has been before the exam. It highlights gaps in certain areas and indicates how much thought has been given before the exam day. Poor preparation would inevitably be reflected in the finished piece of academic writing.

Effective Note-Taking and Information

During the study and revision period, having a more efficient note and study material is a key to achieving top grades during an exam. The difficulty in remembering is not due to poor brain but to poor information management and note-taking. As students, we tend to gather more information than we really need in an attempt to remember enough for the exam (memorise it all), a procedure which is counterproductive and leads to information overload. Remember, it is never about how much you can write in an examination but rather how necessary the information you have written is to the topic in question. Too much information is neither smart nor beneficial on exam day.

First of all, find out exactly what the exam might consist of before you begin your note-taking. This will help in the decision of what information is likely necessary. Effective note-taking means filtering the information you need from the information you don't. Focus on quality rather than quantity. Finding the right balance between too much information and too little is a matter of practice and understanding what is expected of you in the exam. At times, just an appreciation of critical concepts might suffice. At other times, more words are needed to explain specific concepts in order to remember them better.

But how do we take useful notes? The answer depends on the subject involved. However, as a general rule of thumb, reading and comprehending material is vital before note-taking. The idea is to reduce time and effort in writing down only what is considered relevant to your exam. So before taking notes for exam study, students should read around the subject area as much as possible to ascertain what's relevant to take note of for later revision. This is also a build-up of better judgment in managing note-taking.

Effective note-taking is just one of the ways to achieve top grades. Practices such as an organised study routine and other foundational and procedural approaches are also vital.

Note-taking

The last few days before an exam should be spent going through your revision notes rather than making more notes or cutting down on already-written notes. Study notes should not be too large or too small; there should be a balance of what is relevant and necessary. A dilemma you might find yourself in is that your notes seem smaller than they should be. But examiners are not looking for lengthy essays in exams; what they are interested in is the quality of your work and how much engagement, originality, and preparation has been poured into it.

Note-taking is therefore all about cutting down the information you've been given to a manageable quantity. You don't have enough time to reread the voluminous materials over and over again before the examination. If at the end of the day you still have too much information to process efficiently, you are not exercising enough discretion at the initial stage. In fact, the process of figuring out what the important points are and why is what learning is all about.

I once took an exam, studied really hard for it, and put in my very best. Two of my answers were shorter than my first answer, because I knew much on the first one; however, when I got my result back, I got a high mark. This showed me that examiners value quality over quantity. Making your essays more concise permits examiners to see the main points they are looking for without having to go through a painful process of puzzles to find them.

Your note-taking, revision habits, and general study skills are all interlinked with the outcome of your grades. As later chapters will indicate, having a well-structured study schedule is critical in achieving top grades during exams. Last-minute cramming and poor sleeping patterns are counterproductive and should be avoided at all cost.

Practice Effective Essay Writing

The most important part of your exam is knowledge and application (the write-up). It should be noted that while examiners are interested in your capacity to demonstrate what experience and knowledge you have acquired throughout the relevant academic period, they are also interested in your answer or your essay. In most cases, essay questions are posed with a word like *discuss, evaluate, provide,* or *apply*. They are simply asking you to demonstrate in an essay fashion your competence in knowledge and application of the subject matter. Therefore, to achieve top marks, you should practice better essay writing.

Essay writing is a full topic on its own and therefore beyond the scope of this book. However, some suggestions can be derived, as this chapter aims to unfold the critical fundamentals in arriving at top-grade essays. Essay writing requires a high degree of detail, and a good essay should show a high level of knowledge and understanding in precise, concise fashion. Each essay question has some unique language, giving it an additional sign of competence in knowledge and application. For instance, applying the right subject vocabulary is a powerful way of showing the examiner what you are capable of. It demonstrates that you are richly familiar with the subject in discussion and can apply your knowledge accordingly to give your essay distinctive merits.

Students should be advised to start with an introduction (definition) and then move on to discussion, evaluation, and conclusion. Remember, your goal is not only to show the examiners that you know what they want you to explain but also that you can apply that knowledge in the right places within the time frame. It is difficult to attain a top grade in an exam without showing evidence of an excellent essay. A student who fails to achieve top marks is considered to have not met relevant criteria to earn them. The student's write-up failed to demonstrate coherent flow, preparation, understanding, and knowledge in a logical and coherent manner. The student didn't filter the information well enough to retain just the relevant bits.

A drag-and-drop essay tells the examiner you have not prepared adequately; you have just memorised vital concepts. While this demonstrates familiarity with the subject, it also shows lack of a deeper understanding and critical evaluation. Your essay should have an introduction, discussion, evaluation points, critique, and conclusion. Other examples can be found in research papers, journal articles, and written dissertations. If you can get this framework right, you are on your way to top marks.

CHAPTER 7

Memory and Remembering

*Memory is a student's best friend, even if it fails us
sometimes or all the time, we never stop relying on it.*

While the previous chapters focused on accountability, responsibility, time management, learning style, preparation, the burden of academic competence, scenarios of exam results, and attaining top grades, those top grades are only achievable if we know how memory works and how we can utilise it to our advantage during exams. A basic understanding of the role of memory is therefore considered relevant.

Despite being intelligent, motivated and hard-working, most students still struggle to remember much after hours of studying for an exam. One plausible explanation is that the information they want to retain has not made it into the long-term memory bank. Students are unable to present what they have studied for in an exam condition if they can't recall vital information, and they are unable to recall crucial pieces of information if such information hasn't made its way from short-term memory into long-term memory.

As this chapter will reveal, understanding the basics of memory could foster a more efficient way of learning and remembering. The literature on memory is quite extensive and still growing, and this book lacks the space and full capacity to detail its nature. However, it provides readers with a basic blueprint of what memory is all about and how students can utilise a fundamental knowledge of the process of memory to their advantage in preparation for an exam.

It is challenging to excel and produce a top grade in an exam if students are not provided with the understanding of specific fundamental primary processes of how the human memory works. This is because in most cases, exam questions are not simply based on the application of common sense, logic, or general knowledge but on an understanding of the subject area, the specific application of knowledge, facts, figures, dates, etc.

Students who have excellent memory recall during an exam are able to demonstrate clarity and coherency in expression and application of knowledge, all of which are important to the examiner when assessing a student's level of competence during their marking. It follows that, while adequate reading and studying are essential for an exam, at times the problems commonly faced by students are not due to lacking time to learn or study or not having learned enough; instead, the problem is not being able to remember enough from what they have studied before the actual exam.

There's no point in reading extensively and rigorously if we can't remember what we have revised in the exam. Apart from gadgets, learning apps, and other complicated filing systems for keeping our study materials organised, our memory is also important and should take priority in preparation for an upcoming exam. This is because, while learning is critical to exam performance, remembering is just as valid and vital.

It is essential to understand that memory only occurs when we have formed a link with the study material and revised in such a way that it passes through our short-term memory into our long-term memory for successful recollection (a process called encoding). This chapter, therefore, aims to deliver a specific fundamental process of how memory works and how we as students can make our studying more efficient for better memory recall.

Memory

Research suggests that we have to be interested in something to remember it well. For example, we have no problem recalling our favourite movie, character names, artists, footballers, etc. We can also consider the fact that reoccurrence of these details of interest on a daily or weekly basis also plays a role in how well and efficiently we can recollect them.

In essence, interest alone can't guarantee recollection of specific facts, but the additional element of reoccurrence (repetition) can. For the purpose of exams, *interested* could mean showing attentiveness to specific pieces of information we want to remember to recall them better or make sense of them. Reoccurrence of the information in whatever form presented could be considered as conscious, deliberate repetition, equivalent to maintenance rehearsal. Conscious, deliberate repetition in this sense is a purposeful act whereby students regularly expose themselves to and engage with material on more than one occasion, in an attempt to familiarise themselves with the information.

Sensory Register, Short-Term Memory, and Long-Term Memory

Students who have had the chance to study disciplines related to human anatomy, such as biology or psychology, would know that memory consists of sensory register, short-term memory (STM), and long-term memory (LTM)—all distinguishable by their capacity to retain information for a different period of time.

The information we learn is considered to be held in the sensory register through one of the senses (eyes, nose, fingers, or tongue) and also depending on which side of the brain is involved (left hemisphere or hemisphere). As mentioned above, attention/interest is critical to enable the information to move from our sensory register to our STM, as attention is considered to be the first step in remembering.

To enable any information to move from our STM to our LTM, we need to receptively rehearse the piece of information we aim to remember, otherwise we are more likely to lose it. Also, because our STM is limited in capacity to store data, on occasions where we fail to transfer the information learned before we take in fresh information, we automatically lose the previous information. Since there is limited space to take in more information, new information overrides old information.

Repetition is thought to strengthen information that passes through the STM into the LTM, a process called *maintenance rehearsal*. Repetition/ rehearsal not only strengthens the knowledge but enables the information to be remembered when we try to access it.

Understanding

Good recollection involves understanding the vital piece of information you wish to remember. Therefore, your aim during revision is to prioritise understanding over memorisation. You want to transfer any essential information into your LTM. As students, we should bear in mind that it is easier to understand certain concepts and critical facts through understanding the information they are attached to than to memorise them in isolation. I have come across students who have attempted to abbreviate large chunks of data or shorthand them in an attempt to memorise the whole bunch. They later find out that they can't remember that piece of information when required off the top of their head.

Memorising a key concept does not guarantee later recollection. It should follow that understanding is crucial and a critical factor in ensuring that the piece of information we are trying to remember moves smoothly into our long-term memory. Students who simply skim through information run the risk of not being able to move the information from their STM into their LTM. This is particularly true for complex data.

In his book *Smarter Faster Better*—which I would recommend to any student—Charles Duhigg states that "we live in a time when data is more plentiful, cheaper to analyse, and easier to translate into action than ever before. Smartphones, websites, digital databases, and app put information at our fingertips. But it only becomes useful if we know how to make sense of it." In essence, it is only useful if we can understand it.

How do we know how to use a piece of information? The answer is rather simple and obvious and can be extracted from the above: by understanding it. Sometimes as students, we have fallen into the habit of not delegating the responsibility to our brain to remember things better for future retrieval. This is because we rely too much on portable external storage means that enable us to retrieve information on demand. With the aid of smartphones and tablets, we can call upon information with a single click without having to remember it or think about it much. Facts are readily accessible and mobile.

These habits interfere with our ability to retrieve information when we don't have access to the media we are so used to using as an aid. During an exam, remembering is what matters most. One of the best ways to reduce the occurrence of forgetting is to remember better. If this is the case, how can we remember better? We have to make it a mental habit to remind ourselves to remember what we need to remember (maintenance rehearsal). Make it an objective to think it over, wherever you are, and silently remember. How often we learn what we learn has an impact on how often we remember what we have discovered.

CHAPTER 8

Significance of Forgetting and Exams

Forgetting is the antidote to forgetting

When it comes to an exam, forgetting is often thought of as a negative. We become anxious and restless when we can't remember a piece of vital information. Is it because we have gaps in knowledge? Are we just not genetically predisposed to remember much? Or is it merely because we haven't given adequate attention to the possibility of forgetting?

A plausible answer is that before using the information, we haven't given adequate attention to the possibility of forgetting. Oddly enough, forgetting aids remembering. It is what helps us remember a large but efficient piece of information. While students are often advised to incorporate specific learning techniques—such as spaced repetition—to increase the level of recall in an exam condition, a student is often not told how to secure a memory long enough to use it during an exam.

Psychologically speaking, the concept of *forgetting* is beyond the scope of this book. However, understanding its primary fundamental element is important for sitting an actual exam and maintaining top grades. This chapter highlights how forgetting can help students store information more efficiently for exams and provides a logical explanation of why forgetting is good. Furthermore, it proposes adopting a learning technique such as maintenance rehearsal. As part of the revision routine, this chapter encourages students to cover the possibility of forgetting. In essence, forgetting is a critical factor in remembering before an exam.

Take, for example, a diary. We might have about twenty different dates of events, interviews, and meetings we need to attend. We store this information in our journal to aid memory because we are more likely to forget some if not most of it due to daily life events. As humans, we sometimes forget; it is in our nature, in our DNA. We need a reminder, some constant reassurance. As much as necessary, we review our diary in an attempt to ensure that we don't miss any events or meetings. We keep a log because we know we have a vital piece of information we need to remember before its due date. We keep going back to the diary to keep track of the information, and on the day, we remember it.

Now let's take an academic scenario: We have gathered the relevant revision materials, done the research, drawn up a study schedule, created a conducive study cave, read the recommended textbooks, and gone through supplementary materials. We know the subject areas for the exam by now. We've studied really hard—really really hard. The exam day comes, we view the questions, we pick the ones we want to write about, and we begin. We write, and fifteen minutes into the whole ordeal, we stop and think, unable to recall. We can't remember the facts, concepts, dates, times, and places. Our memory fails us at the crucial time.

While it is impossible to remember every single piece of information that has been taught during an academic period, it is possible to remember everything we have taken note of to remember during the exam. Part of the reason for this is that the ability to read and understand is one thing; the capacity to remember is another when it comes to the actual exam day. It should follow that students who learn and space out the learning, so they have breaks in between, then revisit the learning materials again, try to recall/forget, then repeat again, are more likely to retain the information they wish to remember during an exam—provided they have followed a well-structured revision schedule and taken useful notes.

As readers can probably guess, forgetting is all too common during an exam. Our memory can be unreliable at times. At a critical moment, like during an exam, we can't afford to forget the vital information that would bump our marks up enough to reflect our effort. Before the exam, we seem to assume we will remember all the revised information; during the exam we find out we can't. But why? One of the main reasons is that we forget to remember before it is important not to forget. Forgetting in itself is a technique for learning and better recollection of information. Revision is meaningless if a student can't recall half or most of it during the exam.

Benedict Carey, in his book *How We Learn,* stated that "forgetting a chunk of what we've just learned, especially when it's a brand-new topic, is not necessarily evidence of laziness, attention deficits, or a flawed character.

On the contrary, it is a sign that the brain is working as it should." So don't panic when you forget. Your brain is fine. You just need some insight as to how to react and use forgetting as a remembering aid before it's too late. The brain is believed to have unlimited storage capacity, and we are able to hold as much data in our long-term memory. However, we don't want or need much information; we only need the most relevant information.

Going from Negative to Positive with Forgetting

While forgetting is generally viewed as a negative concept, a bad sign of poor memory or dementia, the opposite can be true, as briefly explained above. When a piece of information is stored in our brain through encoding (visually, acoustically, or semantically), at times we remember it in an instant when needed, but at other times (during an exam, for example), we can't remember it when we need it the most.

Forgetting is what increases the probability and certainty that we will not forget most if not all the relevant information required for a specific exam. It strengthens the retrieval strength of particular information in our memory and fosters retrieval on demand. However, timing is crucial. Forget before the exam (during revision), not during the exam (under time pressure).

Students who struggle to remember much during the exam do so because before the exam day, they have failed to forget what they are now trying so hard to remember. I once revised for three days, and after the isolating tedious and cumbersome revision, I understood the topic, but I couldn't remember the key facts (names, dates, concepts) as often as I would like. I started panicking because I couldn't remember the relevant information that would push my marks up. I practically forgot it. I said to myself, *This is bad!* In fact, it was the opposite. It was good! It gave me a different perspective on forgetting and encouraged this chapter. I forgot to remember what was relevant, and then I reviewed my memory and reread the concepts/facts until I was able to remember them when it was relevant (exam day).

When we forget earlier on during our revising, it means we have identified an issue early, before it is too late. Forgetting is one of the most powerful influences on learning. It prompts us to revisit specific facts again and again (repetition) until we are satisfied we have got it. Forgetting can be thought of as playing an advisory role. Forgetting highlights a need to revisit and rehearse the information we can't remember.

While the brain is capable of absorbing and storing a large quantity of data, forgetting is considered a spam filter in the sense that it ensures that we are only retrieving what we want, given the situation, out of all we have stored in our memory. It limits the amount of irrelevant information we need at a particular moment. However, we don't want the brain to assume specific information is irrelevant when it is actually relevant for the exam questions we wish to answer.

In the previous chapter, it was stated that once the information we need gets into the LTM, it stays there, and we can access it even after an extended period. Why is it that at times we can't remember something we need to, when we have deliberately committed it to memory? Why can't we access the information? Is it gone from our memory? Why do we suddenly remember after long deliberate thinking or subsequent rehearsal? There is a considerable body of research on why we forget, and it is largely explored in psychology.

This chapter touches on fundamental concepts in their basic form to help you as a student understand the value of forgetting before your upcoming exams. When we forget, we are unable to recall relevant information which we have learned and now need to remember. Forgetting is a motivator for remembering. During studies before an exam, we might sometimes find ourselves unable to remember a crucial fact or concept we have just gone through. We become uncertain about it, and we end up going back to it again, to the critical concept or material. Once we recheck it, the answer hits us straight away.

Some students fail to remember specific relevant critical concepts during an exam because they haven't taken the time to check up on what they might forget. Therefore, a few days before the exam, always check fundamental concepts you wouldn't want to forget during the exam. The art of forgetting is one way to communicate better with your memory. It connects the dots. It forces you to pay particular attention to something you have to remember. It forces you to remember better. Once you understand some basic principles of forgetting, you will find that nothing is impossible to remember. It is always immensely reassuring when we remember something which we couldn't before.

But Why Do We Actually Forget?

Interference

One explanation provided by researchers to explain forgetting is that at times, one memory disrupts another. While you are trying to recall one piece of information, you end up remembering another piece rather than the one you are working so hard to remember. New learning could interfere with previously learned material (retroactive interference) or prior learning could interfere with what you are trying to learn now (proactive interference).

Retrieval Failure

At times, the reason we can't remember specific information is that we don't have anything around us at that particular moment to remind us. The information we need is in our memory. However, it is not accessible because of the absence of a clue to help us remember. It follows that forgetting in the LTM is due to retrieval failure. While the information is available, we can't seem to access it due to no association to something that might trigger the memory.

Research suggests that one way to remember something is to find a cue—something to trigger that memory. A cue can be used as a reminder that somehow connects what we want to remember to what can be used to remember it. When it comes to an exam, this has limited applicability. The exam consists of a lot of information, and a cue would be needed for each piece if we were to utilise this method.

Encoding Failures

Is the information we need to remember adequately encoded? Encoding describes the process of how information is processed so that it can be stored in our memory. Except for neurological problems such as amnesia or dementia, or the influence of specific medications, our brain is capable of retention and recollection of key relevant information needed for higher performance during an exam. One reason we might be said to forget what we have learned is due to an encoding failure.

Encoding failure is reported to occur because the information we are trying to retrieve from our memory is currently not available. It has not been successfully transferred and stored in LTM. No matter how hard we try to remember the piece of information we now wish to recall, we struggle and fail because it has not passed through STM into LTM. It slipped away before it got the chance to move into LTM storage.

Retrieval Strength

The speed at which we can remember any piece of information depends on its retrieval strength. Any memory we store in our brain is never lost. It might seem to be gone, but with the right cues and usage, we tend to remember it. A fundamental fact to remember is that to forget is not due to the absence of a memory or a piece of information but the lack of strength in retrieving that memory. Retrieval strength relies on usage. The more you use it, the stronger it gets; the less you use it, the weaker it gets. The frequency at which we use any information strengthens the speed at which we can remember it. The more we use the data, the more we have it readily available. Accessibility becomes automatic. There are certain things we can recall in a heartbeat.

When we forget a name and somehow later remember it, that memory grows stronger, making us less likely forget the name again. For instance, we don't forget our own name. Why? Because we use it often when we introduce ourselves to people, when we fill out various forms, present our IDs, etc. When we forget a piece of information, we most likely have to think hard to remember it. Once we recall it, the retrieval strength of remembering that same piece of information becomes much quicker.

Maintenance Rehearsal

What do we do when we discover that we can't remember specific information? Rehearse the information again. Maintenance rehearsal is suggested as an effective method when using forgetting to our advantage before an exam. Maintenance rehearsal involves the active repetition of a piece of information again and again. When we go over a piece of information, particularly one we have initially forgotten, we eventually create a better retrieval strength in LTM for later retrieval. It also prompts us to give more attention to the information we are trying to retrieve.

CHAPTER 9

Discipline and Habits

Discipline is the pillar upon which success is built
and upon which success remains standing.

In this chapter, you will learn about the benefit of having excellent disciplined study habits. Good study habits are fundamentals for exam preparation. Students who lack discipline in practical application often find themselves drifting emotionally and mentally when placed under exam stress. Excellent study habits are paramount during the exam period. They convey a level of discipline capable of helping you develop resilience under stress and pressure during revision and study periods.

Disciplined study habits combine three things: your thoughts, your emotions, and your behaviours. All three influence your performance and results. Thoughts such as

- *I feel like not doing anything today.*
- *I don't care.*
- *It is my teacher's job to teach me all I need to know.*
- *I will leave it all to the last minute.*

are those of a poor-performing student who is either uninformed, unmotivated, or simply uninterested. Acknowledging and understanding good study habits will help you achieve excellent results academically, personally, and even socially.

Discipline and Exams

Discipline involves obeying certain strict rules and regulations and imposing punishment when these are not followed. Rules in the academic sense include sticking to proper study techniques and following good study habits and teacher instructions. This ensures stability and consistency in performance and result. Punishment in this sense would be poor academic achievement, a consequence of failing to adhere to good study practices.

Theodore Roosevelt once said, "With self-discipline most anything is possible." More recently, Jim Rohn claimed, "Discipline is the bridge between goals and accomplishment." And Robert Kiyosaki asserted that "Confidence comes from discipline and training." All three prominent individuals are consistent in their opinion that discipline is the backbone of progress and is therefore vital to any level of achievement. With the right level of discipline, any academic result can be obtained and maintained.

Discipline in this sense means sticking to a specific guided routine no matter what. Apply discipline to when you study, what you study, and how you put studying first before anything else. Repeat all of the above, over and over again, until you get it done. Discipline, in essence, is maintaining a repeated behaviour without wavering; without fretting unnecessarily; without losing focus, commitment, and control; and without losing yourself.

An excellent study habit can be categorised as a useful academic action a student engages in that leads to a progressive result. Habits carried out in a lazy way can lead to a complete breakdown in progress. Habits are like traps, and when we fall into them, we end up limited, restrained, and unable to move forward academically. We simply stop progressing. The more we approach our academic affairs in a certain way, the more automatic that becomes. Habits are said to be what we repeatedly do.

Our daily engagement with our studies says a lot about our habits. Some students study a few hours a day, sleep well at night, and wake up full of energy—upbeat, driven, and with a can-do attitude. Other students wake up tired, with a sneer of disengagement and a sense of cluelessness, because they stayed awake at night studying last minute for hours in one session. As the day progresses, they begin to experience exhaustion and complacency in class.

Revision sessions for these exhausted students might have been extensive in quantity but not in quality. They might have left their revision till the last minute and tried to cram it all in at once by doing an all-nighter. They might have read a psychology book of 360 pages rather than focused on the questions which might come up in the exam. Conclusively, it would follow that due to poor study routines or habits, they fail to perform adequate research or sufficient preparation on what to study. Therefore, the number of hours they have done would not correspond with the effort they have put in.

Without good practices, it will be virtually impossible to achieve excellent grades. Good habits breed excellence. A key principle is that habits are behaviours driven by thoughts and emotions and exposed through action. The best way to manage habits is to control them. To ensure specific outcomes such as top grades, exceptional academic or personal performance, and results, you must maintain specific behaviour through certain habits. Discipline is a decision to take action until a particular object is obtained. This is precisely where control comes into play. Discipline at the end of the semester entails commitment and control.

Students should be advised that the first step to a good habit is acknowledging the distinction between good and bad habits and analysing and comparing them with their study habits. They should understand that good habits do not take root overnight but gradually, through the reinforcement of good, conscious, deliberate repetition. You have to apply self-control, start small, do more study, attend more classes, and aim higher.

The majority of things we do on a daily basis are habit-driven behaviours, which at some point have become automatic, routine, and uncontrollable. However, as students, we need control over how we conduct our academic activities. At times, our habits can have a detrimental effect on the outcome of our grades. Such habits include the following:

- choosing to watch TV over studying
- skimming textbooks rather than consciously and diligently reading them
- skipping classes rather than attending them
- copying other people's work rather than expanding your own
- keeping quiet in class and not asking important questions
- missing out on the opportunity to contribute among your peers
- failing to stick to the reading list
- failing to buy the relevant study materials or textbook

To succeed, we must change these automatic behaviours into deliberate conscious behaviours through a controlled pattern of habit.

Good Habits

Not long ago, I was helping a friend who was about to take his maths exam. We had spent three hours on his revision materials the day before.

On the way out of the library, he was over the moon. He said, "Samson, this is the first time I have ever studied for three hours!"

I was speechless and shocked! He had gone through preschool, high school, and college, and he hadn't studied more than three hours before? I asked out of curiosity, "How long do you normally study for?"

"Thirty minutes maximum throughout the week, every now and then," he answered.

I told him he needed to go over his study habits, apply more time and discipline in his study routine, and apply better organisation to his study materials (they were all over the place). Having a learning style is only useful when we can utilise it in a disciplined way. If we have a disciplined study habit where we can put in a few hours each day on trying to study or recall anything we want to learn, our cognitive processing will improve in speed, adapt to our learning style, and improve recollection. The following are examples of good study habits.

Finding a Study Pack

One way to keep up good study habits is to find or create a study group that contributes meaningfully to what you are studying for. I remembered sitting in the library sometimes and noticing a group of students gathered together with various books opened in front of them, each deeply into it in a disciplined way. As a collective ritual, they were scribbling, underlining, highlighting, or tracing words with their fingers. Another time, I would see them chatting, giggling, and laughing, while avoiding the thick books and scattered papers in front of them.

During mock exams, they seemed to obtain higher grades, and in a common consistency. It was here I understood why students who are considered smart remain smart. They are always in a pack when they study, like wolves—smart packs of wolves. They operate together at a specific given time, attacking their gaps in knowledge, filling them up with the knowledge they have accumulated and retrieved from books, and then comparing what they have learned.

One day, I sat a little closer to their table, and I noticed that the chatting was actually questioning. One of the students would hurl a question towards the rest of the pack, who in turn would attempt to deliver the correct answer. I realized they were testing themselves, trying to recollect the answers to the question for when they had to do the mock or the actual exam. They were preparing in advance by sharing knowledge and exploring understanding, while at the same time hanging around with fellow smart students.

Group study is one way to stay up to date with your subjects. You can ask questions from different angles and consider answers from different mind-sets.

Contributing in Class

It is paramount that you stand out in class and show your teachers that you can work individually as well as in a team. Show that you can move a lesson or lecture forward by contributing. Speaking up in class has the advantage of reinforcing the belief that you know the stuff which you should know. It is another way of attempting to recollect concepts and facts. This is an unconscious way of recollection.

One of the advantages I have had is that I always make it a point to speak up in class, raise my hand, and contribute when given the go-ahead. I used to sit with a classmate who always knows the answer. He whispered it in my ear sometimes when it seemed like no one else could answer it, just to show me that he knew more. One day I asked him, "Patrick, why don't you raise your hand as everyone does and answer the question so everyone knows you know the answer?"

He gave a lazy shrug and said he never raised his hand in class. He was too ashamed to. He thought that his accent was laughable, and he almost always gave the wrong answer anyway.

I looked him in the eye and said, "When your hunger to learn is greater than your pride and ego, you begin to feel an absence of embarrassment and a presence of reckless boldness regardless of how laughable it would sound when you, in front of your peers, say, 'I don't know the answer, but I want to know.'"

Minimising the Impact of Stress

Exam stress is unavoidable, but it can be controlled. Given the inevitable nature of exam stress and fear, how you manage the stress level is down to how well prepared you have been throughout the process leading to the exam. No matter how prepared I was, I still felt a little sense of anxiousness before the exam, even when my revision had been rigorously carried out. I have concluded that it is the fear of the unknown rather than the fear of being unprepared. It is a natural human reaction and nothing more.

However, many students do fear exams because their revision period lacks the proper preparation in time and quality. For instance, some students leave their exam revision until the very last minute—and I mean a day or two before the exam. While at times such an attitude could get you a lucky pass, it doesn't always work, and in the long run, it is likely to fail you.

Students who leave their revision until the last minute experience a lot of panic and anxiety prior to and after their exams, making it difficult to concentrate and manage other post-exam studies. A key tip is to get ahead and stay ahead in your revision. Have an organised system in place; for example, keep a journal to track things like dates of exams, study times, resources to look into (like textbooks and revision guides), and personal notes.

Getting Enough sleep

Sufficient sleep during the study process is essential. To maintain alertness, students are encouraged to pursue adequate sleep throughout the process. According to research, lack of sleep (including attempting to pull an all-nighter) before the exam day has a negative effect on how we perform during exams. Some students feel they are at their best at night when everyone else is sleeping, because they benefit from the solitude and absence of interruptions, demands, errands, and noise. However, this does affect their day in class. They feel sleepy and drowsy, at times even nodding off in the classroom. Students who find that night-time is the only time they are able to focus should seek advice from their teachers or parents on how they can be helped.

During the exam period, apart from drowsiness in the days leading up to the exam, lack of sleep has other counterproductive repercussions. Sleep-deprived students are like loose cannons during exam periods. They don't sleep several days before the exam day, and their mind begins to run in all directions. Their brain becomes inefficient and unpredictable in terms of how much it can store for later recollection. They stay up all night, locked up in libraries, and attempt to stay awake through various unhealthy means. They are then exposed to the side effects of sleep deprivation, including lack of alertness, stress, and mental breakdown—all leading to forgetfulness during the exam.

While such students might have studied hard in a sleepless state, their overall performance on exam day will be less efficient, and their intellectual performance will be limited, resulting in a lower grade than they deserve. Lack of sleep doesn't just make you drowsy; it reduces concentration, memory storage, and later recollection. Memory is an integral part of taking an exam. A student has to be alert enough to take the required information in and store it in such a way that it goes through the STM to the LTM.

Research illustrates that lack of sleep can affect brain neurons. For instance, studies show that when mice are deprived of sleep and forced to stay awake longer than usual, they begin to develop neuron loss, which in the long term causes brain damage along with reduction in memory storage. Improve your study habits to reduce such risks.

CHAPTER 10

Exam-SMART

The best way to get to a destination quicker is to weigh the routes smartly and ensure that the chosen path is the best possible option available.

The preceding chapters have already suggested certain key habits to implement. This chapter will expand on one very crucial principle: being Exam-SMART. It is no coincidence that at times, students feel stressed throughout their exam preparation, unable to keep track of the amount of information they have studied or the time they have left. Students are always worried that they will not have time to cover enough topics before the exam. They become eager to get studying out of the way with little preparation and no plan. They set themselves unrealistic and irrelevant goals that are later revealed to be unachievable, short on structure and clarity, and without specific destination. Studying becomes unachievable with this approach.

These students' study routine is chaotic, unorganised, and without the necessary discipline. It lacks smartness. What the Exam-SMART approach provides is a more structured study experience and a way to measure progress. Students who implement Exam-SMART strategies can evaluate their study progress and perform better than other students. They are advised to set a deadline a few days before exam day—at least three or four days before—similar to an actual essay hand-in deadline. This provides them with enough wiggle room to address specific untouched information which might be relevant.

What is Exam-SMART? It is a study tool that enables students to track their study progress at any given time. The acronym SMART, credited to George T. Doran, is usually used in a business setting as a useful tool for setting goals, assessing them, and achieving them efficiently with less effort and less time. The acronym is made up of the following:

- *S* for *specific*
- *M* for *measurable*
- *A* for *achievable*
- *R* for *relevant*
- *T* for *timely*

Exam-SMART applies this by coordinating your study time, study mind, and study goals so that at the end of the study day, you can trace your study back and measure your current level of progress. Students who implement the Exam-SMART strategy during an exam can contain the otherwise chaotic stress that exam preparation would otherwise bring. Let us consider each of these SMART elements as they apply to exams.

Exam-Specific

When students ask me anything to do with exam revision and studies, I usually reply with a question: "What is your objective, your goal, your finish line?"

They generally just stare at me silently, their mind blank.

I charge on. "Are you aiming for a higher grade or just a pass?"

Their answer to this question clears up any uncertainty I might have concerning what they want to get out of a session with me. Without a specific goal, you only have luck to rely on. For the purpose of an exam, a specific approach should be split into two elements: an objective and crucial information.

Objective

An objective is the most crucial element of any action, for it carries a sense of value or justification. It forces you to ask, *Why am I doing it? Why should I do it? Is it a necessity, a benefit, or for the purpose of reward?* Your objective is your primary goal. It is a conscious act of stating where your finish line should be. How far should your effort reach: to a higher grade, a swift transition into the next academic stage, or an overall outstanding educational qualification?

Before we go any further, imagine this: Your country is aggressively snowed-up, cold, rainy, and windy. You want to visit a country without cold, wind, rain, snow, or any sight of grey and moody clouds. Your goal is to find someplace with tropical weather where you can simply enjoy the summer. You make a grown-up decision to just pack and go—no announcement, no invitation, no company, no farewell, no face-to-face goodbyes. This will be a silent journey, just you and yourself, for pure needed solitude.

Imagine further that you decide to choose your destination by writing six different countries down on six different little cut-out papers, one colour each. You squeeze each one with your hand into a small ball before putting it into your palm. You then fold your palm into a fist. You rattle the balls of paper around your curled palm before opening it and picking out one, unopened. You then chucked the remaining paper balls in your wastepaper basket.

With no knowledge of which destination you picked, you pack your luggage. With no knowledge of which destination you picked, you took traveling documents and headed to the airport with your unopened piece of paper. How confident are you that you will end up with a country you really would like to go to? How confident are you that you have the necessary documents to get there? Keep imagining and playing this scenario out before you start any academic studies. Imagine you found out the conclusion of this little story. I did: it was a shambles.

Students who operate without an objective engage in a similar play of luck—a game of pass or fail, nothing in-between, nothing exceeding it. They fancy themselves in a game of chance, and like a roulette player, they gamble away, spinning round and round. They flirt with ambiguity and most likely end up in as much of a shambles as that impetuous traveller. They spin on the edge of uncertainty rather than balancing at the centre where the goal is more defined and there is clarity between focus and intention, intention and objective, and performance and result.

Students are therefore advised to begin with a clear end goal in mind. Have an objective before you start your studies or any revision. Ask yourself, *What do I want to get out of my revision today? What specific grade am I aiming for in the forthcoming exam?* An objective carries with it a degree of certainty that enables you to know that what you are working on will inevitably lead to what you are aiming for.

In essence, objectives eliminate ambiguity and provide a sense that we are on the right path—that we are going toward something we really want. There are no ifs or buts or maybes, only certainty in the outcome. We have departed for and will arrive at our desired destination.

Crucial Information

Specification is all about asking direct questions and proposing unambiguous, clear answers—and getting close to the fact as much as possible when it comes to an exam. The more you know about the exam, the better you can prepare for it. Your questions might include the following:

- What are the subjects involved?
- How many are there?
- Are there any gaps between the exam dates?
- How many past papers are available?
- What grades do I want to achieve?
- Are these internal exams or external exams?
- How long will the exam be?
- What SMART goals can I set?
- Who do I need to see if I need some help?
- Where do I want to study?
- What materials do I need?

Specifics reduce uncertainty and assumptions that might end up being false or misleading. They make your time more productive and keep you focused when you get going.

Exam-Measurable

Right from the first day of each semester, I always seek to know when the exam dates are. This breaks the study process down to manageable components from the outset. I usually use a schedule table, such as the one at the end of this book, to make a note of my exam dates and other relevant information. Other times, I write the information down on sticky notes and stick them on my study desk where I can see them as often as necessary. At least once a week, I double-check. I have learned the need for this the hard way.

Once, I thought I had enough time to cover three different exams. I thought they were further apart from each other, giving me time to include all three. It turned out they were only days apart. For at least two years now, from the start, I make it a deliberate behaviour to think about each exam's date, subject area, potential questions, and deadlines. This has enabled me to make sure my revision plan is done in advance: when I want to start, how long I wish to spend on each subject, which ones are the hardest and require more time, and how far exams are from each other.

I examine this information and ask myself: *Do I have sufficient time for studying and for revision? Can I do more social activities, or do I need to cut down? Have I got any important events that might overlap with my revision days or my exam day that I need to address and adjust?* If I think of anything else, I review, add, change, recheck, and confirm. This should be an ongoing project before study and revision days start.

Exam-Achievable

Prior to exam revision, think about what grade you want to achieve. Remember the earlier section about objectives: top grade or graduation? Determine the result are you aiming for: first class? second class? third? Whatever that might be, you should know from the start and work with your given target in mind.

Right at the start, ask yourself whether your objective grade is subjectively attainable. Think in terms of what *you* think you are capable of, not what anybody else thinks. Be honest with yourself. Don't ambush yourself by setting unrealistic goals that you can't currently achieve. You can only grow when you honestly identify your strengths and weaknesses. You can't play yourself; your final written work will betray you if you do. So be honest about what you can currently achieve and what you feel like, if you put your best into it, you would be able to attain by the end of your revision period.

Exam-Relevant

Why do you need this grade? Why is this particular exam relevant to you? For a conditional offer, perhaps? A vocational course or university, college, etc? A future career? To make your parents happy and proud? It has to mean something to you, simply because value drives us to put our best effort into something.

This should be from your point of view, by the way, rather than from others'. While you should consider other people's opinion on this, a goal drives you more when it comes from you, because it involves gratitude. Gratitude, in retrospect, conveys a feeling of pride, improvement, a new sense of competence, and independence.

Exam-Timely

Often, I hear the phrase "Time is money". My best thought about it is that time is the currency of achievement. When people say "Time is money", they mean time is valuable and should be used efficiently and productively. When it comes to exam revision, students should ensure that time is taken into consideration. Each action should be undertaken with a tentative plan. Draw up a revision schedule with all the relevant subjects on it. Set yourself a deadline to cover those subjects before the exam commences.

Time is also important when practicing with past papers before the exam. Students who do practice papers and time themselves are at an advantage over other students during the actual exam. They have practiced relevant essay question and know how much they would be able to write per question.

Deadlines also make time of the essence. Everybody knows that deadlines are what makes most people switch to action, to stress, to pressure, and in extreme cases, to meltdown and breakdown. Install independent deadlines for yourself during the revision period to ensure that you have enough time to review your revision and address any area in need of attention before the actual exam day.

CHAPTER 11

Study HARD

While smart work is helpful and so encouraged, you simply cannot exclude hard work and expect exceptional results.

Throughout my educational life, I have been directed towards hard work in every area of my studies and personal encounters. I have been consistently instructed by my parents to work hard and study hard. I have been encouraged by my teachers to put in the work. My college subject review was a constant indicator and a reoccurring reminder of this stance. I'm sure that most of you have encountered this also at one point or another.

During parent-teacher meetings, it usually came up: "You need to work harder this semester to exceed your below-average grade." This was not a prescription applied only to me, however. My classmates and friends usually shared our academic reviews. They all had the words, "You need to work harder this semester to obtain a higher grade."

Today, with some of the students I help, when I look at their academic review, those same words are written all over it. I have therefore come to the conclusion that our teachers and parents, through personal experience, at one point or another realised that even with the SMART approach, we can only earn something meaningful and exceptional through the application of hard work. In principle, they all understood that this is how valued things are earned: through hard work. From the preceding chapter, which discussed how being Exam-SMART helps students be efficient in preparing for exams, it can be seen that working smart pre-exam is beneficial and efficient.

However, being Exam-SMART does not excuse or exclude working hard in your studies. Studying hard in this regard is equivalent to working hard, and hard work in action is ascribed to the desire to make whatever you are doing merit the result you aim to achieve. Students who work hard and smart develop a competing foresight and approach their revision/study with more expansive forethought. Like SMART, HARD can be thought of as an acronym:

- *H* is for *honestly*
- *A* is for *autonomously*
- *R* is for *resourcefully*
- *D* is for *devotedly*

Students who study HARD become thorough, predictive, primed, and ready to adjust and adapt. For the above-stated reasons, there is a practical need for hard work when knowledge is paramount and success is at stake.

Students assume that when they cut corners, they are working efficiently and smartly. No. Studying smart is what sets you up; studying hard is what drives you forward. Where achieving consistent high grades is the objective, hard work is required. It is inescapable.

According to Jeffrey Preston Bezos, founder, chairman, and CEO of Amazon, "You can work long, hard, or smart but you can't choose two out of three." In simple terms, they all work alongside each other. They are applicable and useful when used together rather than exclusively. It should be added that hard work is not minute work; it requires quantity as well as quality. Hard work can only be carried out with the investment of sufficient time. You find out exactly what is needed (what you need to do), gather the resources (learning materials) and then create a schedule sufficient for covering those materials.

Quality + Quantity = Exceptionality

Students should bear in mind that while hard work can be exhausting, it is also rewarding. Hard work, as we should know, cannot be done in short drops. It has to be applied in a quantity that exceeds the average of what we have been doing all along during the semester.

Note should be taken that wherever there is quality, there is also an invisible quantity buried in the shadows of its making. To arrive at an exceptional result, a student at one point or another would have had to give more of something—more time spent on reading, writing, or academic actives, for example, or more effort staying sharp in class and showing an increasing state of alertness in the classroom. We must increase the quantity of everything we are doing to exceed and go beyond average in what we are aiming to achieve.

General Assumptions

High marks in an exam setting are not achieved by merely studying smart without thinking about studying hard. That would be a cursory approach. Students should appreciate the fact that studying smart and studying hard are on the same side of the table. They go hand in hand. They facilitate each other. They compensate each other. They add up and produce a constant exceptionality in results.

There is a general assumption that "High-grade students are just plain naturally smart. They don't break a sweat. They don't get stressed out. They don't get overworked. They don't have to even read too much. They don't have to work hard. They are just gifted!" Okay, let's hit the pause button right there! Students can accumulate all the recommended learning materials, gather all the relevant information, categorise each subject, and organise information efficiently, neatly, even chronologically. But if they don't put in the work, they will be wasting valuable time and resources, a consequence studying hard is primarily designed to address.

I cringe when students, friends, and family describe me as really smart. I think silently in my head, *You have no idea how hard I work to get things up there in my brain.* I was more determined and more hard-working; I just made it seem effortless by doing it efficiently, combining both hard work and smart work.

Smart students don't just sit at by the pool at a five-star hotel soaking up the hot sun, drinking a cold beverage, talking to peers, and having an adventure. They don't have a wizard wand, a magic pen, or an exceptional memory. They don't just appear on exam day looking composed, calm, and ready to write first-class answers without having studied hard. They have all worked efficiently (as they should). They have prioritised exam revision (as they should), planned smartly (as they should), and executed the plan by studying hard in an efficient manner (as they should).

Benefits of Working Hard

Understanding the benefits of working hard means that you are not just a passive student, like some others who might have taken the exam just to pass. An active student wants to do better and appreciates that a top class grade requires going the extra mile as a student: covering as much ground as possible while maintaining efficiency in academic engagement throughout the whole study and revision process, regardless of any challenges posed.

It is therefore accurate that the combination of smart and hard studying is what makes hard work more bearable, endurable, manageable, efficient, and rewarding. However, setting up an efficient revision plan is where applying Exam-SMART is most useful. Sitting down, studying, maintaining discipline, and commitment is where studying HARD comes in.

While working hard might seem time-consuming, it forces a student to value things differently. Students become more driven, more composed, and more responsive to challenges. They are able to cover various bases and angles before the exam day, and in so doing appreciate their time better and reach the end result, the end goal, the high mark.

Of course, studying HARD is only appropriate when it is not rushed or left as a last-minute activity. That woudn't be studying HARD; that would be studying desperately. Academic standards are becoming ever so challenging, partly because the competition among exceptional students has gone up a few notches. Information has become easier accumulate, analyse, and utilise just by clicking few buttons on a smartphone or other digital gadget. The essence of hard work seems to be diluted and reduced to something negative, like overworking, burning out, and stressing out unnecessarily. However, the contrary is true.

The Analogy

Let's use a smartphone as an analogy. Smartphones are called *smart* because they focus on simplicity and comfort. They make storing and accessing information easy and fast. We might be smart students, but we are not smart phones. We might be able to make smartphones, but we simply cannot become them. We have to have the flexibility to be able to better ourselves through working harder than we are currently able to do.

An example might help: I remember how many journals and articles I had to go through for my specialist essays, projects, exams, etc. It took hard work and smart thoughts and planning to gather the relevant information, then more hard work to analyse, summarise, and apply them as necessary. The only smart way around it was to work hard. And the only way to do exceptionally in all of them was to apply hard work smartly: by thinking smart and making a plan about what's relevant and where and how to obtain it before going on and working hard.

Students should be aware of this simple fact: if you study HARD without an Exam-SMART plan, you are studying hard for nothing. If you merely approach an Exam-SMART plan without putting in the work (studying HARD), you are wasting everything. What studying HARD and SMART allows you to do is demonstrate in-depth coverage during the actual exam. Your exam answers become persuasive, giving your examiner little room to doubt your understanding.

Writing a top-class exam paper or providing an exceptional answer in an exam condition cannot be done without hard work (studying HARD). Effective preparation without an effective execution is useless. However, where an effective execution follows effective preparation, the intended result is exceptionally achieved. At this point, students should see studying HARD as the equivalent of working HARD. You just have to know where to put in the Exam-SMART studying and when working HARD comes into play.

HARD Mindset

Students are advised to implement a mindset that includes the following elements of the HARD acronym, as mentioned earlier.

Study Honestly

One of my primary mottos for improving my academic standard is "exceptionality is the product of honesty." Therefore, the key to making an effective plan work well is to be open and honest with yourself. Students who aim to improve and excel in any given situation should ask themselves questions like the following:

- *Is my current level of knowledge sufficient?*
- *Do I need more help or less—more one-to-one with my teacher?*
- *Am I prepared enough?*
- *Do I have the right study materials, the right study space, the right study friends, the right frame of mind?*

Students who learn better and improve are honest about their gaps in knowledge and accept the feedback and setbacks they encounter. Students don't get rewarded for being smart; they get rewarded for showing improvement through hard work. Hard work stands out in an exam paper; it shows an examiner that a student has done the homework purposefully and adequately. In reference to an exam, honesty is a personal account of your current competence. You can't study HARD if you don't specify the areas you need to focus on.

One of the best ways to grow is through analysing our setbacks and our feedback. Feedback is an asset if one aims to improve academically. I always check back on my previous feedback, highlight what was pointed out to me as an area of opportunity to grow, and implement that in my current development plan. Anything that indicates a third party's opinion on your current academic knowledge—whether it's feedback on your review or a marked paper—is valuable when preparing for future assessments or exams. Whether you agree with the feedback or not, and/or whether it is true or not, utilise it to your advantage by weighing what you have currently achieved against what it says you need to work on.

Study Autonomously (Exercise Control)

Similar to the element of responsibility explained in the previous chapter, autonomy is an asset to have and maintain during exam preparation. We all want to get good grades and go on to earn well doing what we want to do. Autonomy means taking charge and control of everything that relates to your exam study—from the plans you make to the way you implement and execute them. This is a significant part of the exam study process. Students who study HARD put themselves in a position to go above and beyond. They achieve this level of command by exercising control over how they plan, what they plan, and how they execute their plan.

According to research, individuals who assume and exert control over what they do tend to work harder and go above and beyond. They have an advantage; they become more focused, more ambitious, and more unstoppable. They tend to have an *internal locus of control*, a state in which individuals believe that the choices they make will significantly affect the result they produce. Being in control as a student is therefore paramount to getting things done.

When students are in control of what happens around them, they tend to have everything mapped out. They can confront whatever gaps they have in their knowledge and work toward filling those gaps. No one wants to work hard for nothing, and no one works for nothing; we all want that top grade. Students who assume smartness and still struggle to achieve and maintain better grades should be advised that they are either working hard with an ill-prepared plan or not working hard enough—both of which suggest lack of autonomy.

Study Resourcefully

As a student, it is your primary responsibility to be resourceful. It builds up an independent character regardless of whether you are in a private school, grammar school, state school, university, or vocational school. Being resourceful means being proactive with yourself and more productive with your time. It is paramount that you establish what you need before you start your main revision. Is it a new textbook, study space, learning material, exercise? Students who are resourceful are better prepared and can tick more boxes than usual.

Resourceful students should maintain a balance between who they are and what they want. Don't just attempt to gather everything on earth you can get your fingers on just because you want to be productive or proactive; you will only end up being preoccupied with time-wasting information not relevant to your exam. Plus, you will be exhausted from all of it, and you can't be resourceful if you are overwhelmed and tired.

Be smart with your resources. Some students study hard by binge-studying for hours, trying to accumulate numerous study materials in an attempt to cram information in before the exam. During the exam, their written work lacks persuasion and carries no significant meaning. This is unadvisable, counterproductive, and inefficient.

Study Devotedly

Students who are devoted to their study are more serious about doing better in their exams. They prioritise their current need over their current want. They sacrifice things such as procrastination, meaningless social activities, and other routine distractions, such as phones or TV-watching. Exam preparation gets the spotlight—the full focus.

Devoted individuals invest most of their time and energy in something specific. This is part of working hard—the act of sacrificing things you usually wouldn't be able to do without. A devoted life requires commitment and full-time engagement. While it is understandable that as students we might crave simplicity or an easy life, during the exam period, which is temporal, certain sacrifices have to be made. It's like making an investment for the long-term benefit. However, students should bear in mind that studying HARD does not mean getting overworked, avoiding sleep, or burning out. It simply means being efficiently prepared. As we have noted, preparation is a prerequisite for a top grade.

Studying HARD indicates a seriousness about not just passing but achieving a higher mark. It also involves finding the right balance between working smart and working hard and getting into the mindset of someone who is determined and committed. Make your exam come first above everything else in a way that won't affect your health and normal daily routine.

Bear in mind that nothing great comes easy. Devotion does not feel natural at first. Being devoted is not the usual routine for some students, like being ambitious or other old-school terminology. It is cumbersome to stay disciplined, stay focused, avoid distraction, and ignore social media. It is cumbersome "not to"—not to procrastinate, not to engage, not to do the daily routine, not to party, or not to continually hang around with friends. However, where students practice the art of being devoted to their studies, their revision, and the outcome they want, they become automatically dedicated with less effort.

Hard work projects a kind of disciplined mindset. It engages people more with their end goal. A devoted student makes informed choices, and the learning process becomes smoother and more manageable. Even if such students are not motivated, they feel encouraged to continue.

Chapter 12

Study and Revision Stages

Studying starts at the beginning of the semester.
Revision starts at the end of it.

Now that we have learned from previous chapters the importance of working with an Exam-SMART approach and a HARD mindset, we will turn to the actual process leading up to the exam day. This chapter focuses on two critical stages during the exam period: the study stage and the revision stage. These are the areas student struggle with the most.

Two major questions students ask is, "How many hours do I need to study for?" and "When is the best time to start studying?"

The answer I give for the first question is, "The hours you have to put in studying a subject is subjective and depends on numerous factors, including your gap in knowledge, available materials to study or revise with, your personal schedule, your speed at learning, any natural condition, how organised you are, and how easy it is to get to a study spot."

For the second question, I answer, "You start studying at the very beginning of your semester, not halfway through it or at the end of the semester."

The truth is, there is no magic number of hours that guarantee a top class grade, just proven strategies. There are pre-tried systems in place—practical habits that students can adapt to excel and achieve competitive grades—all of which have been explored in this book. Most of this chapter provides students with a distinction between studying and revising and the significance of revising efficiently.

When it comes to exam preparation, it is vital for students to understand the difference between studying and revising, two concepts often interchangeably used in an ill-informed manner. Both concepts are meant to complement each other by carrying them out at different stages but bringing them together at the end of the revision period.

Understanding the distinction between studying and revising can make a significant difference in a student's overall academic performance— particularly in situations where time is of the essence and the quality in written work is of high calibre and paramount to achieving a specific result. Students should be advised that revising is only useful and productive when they have the information already established. The established information should be well researched, organised, and relevant to the exam in question. When you try to revise whatever you see, you are wasting time and contributing to an unnecessary piling up of information in your head.

Studying is a skill in its own right. It helps us develop a mental filter by enabling us to review raw information and outline and isolate the information that is vital and needed from what is unnecessary. It filters out junk and clutter from our revision materials.

Study vs. Revision

At this point, students should understand that the distinction between studying and revising is not apparent. However, practically, they can be differentiated. To study is to familiarise and understand the information you desire to work on for the exam, while revision forms a more in-depth knowledge with the accumulated information in an attempt to enhance your understanding, retain information, and recall the information when required.

The purpose of revising is to devote time and attention to gaining knowledge of an area of interest or relevance. As explained at the beginning of this chapter, revising is generally considered to be taking another look: reviewing, re-examining, re-evaluating, and rereading work to form a more structured understanding and recall.

Studying

For the benefit of exams, the concept called *studying* is best described as an activity which involves closely scrutinising, observing, and selecting vital and relevant information for a specific purpose. Studying is an attempt to establish relevant information from a broader range of information by gathering main points, facts, and critical concepts through scrutinising written knowledge, skimming through it, examining or evaluating it, and then accumulating only that which you intend to add to your memory through effective note-taking for later recall during an actual request for that information in the real exam.

The active process of studying is, therefore, to familiarise yourself with the relevant material you need for an exam and determine which part is related in an attempt to isolate information in preparation for revising, retention, and retrieval. Studying is a prerequisite for revising, but it is a useful technique in its own right. It can be done from the beginning of the semester. Students who are well prepared during the exam revision period are considered to have accumulated relevant information throughout the teaching period by taking practical and relevant notes class by class and organising them for later review, thereby increasing familiarity with the subject matter. Students should bear in mind that familiarisation increases the probability of understanding, storage, and retrieval because it compels us to pay particular attention, maintain focus, and form a connection with what we want to remember specifically for the exam.

Revision

Revision primarily involves engaging with those main points, facts, and critical concepts already accumulated through the act of studying to equip a student with a transparent direct knowledge of a specific subject area, primarily to engage and prepare better for an examination. Students are advised to allot separate time for studying and revision. During the study stage, students should be reading and highlighting information they wish to revise from recommended study materials (core textbooks) as early as possible. This act is intended to determine which piece of information the student might want to concentrate on during the revision stage. Only after students are satisfied that they have picked out all the information they need to study with can they proceed to the next stage: revising.

During the revision stage, students are advised to review the materials already isolated for that purpose. At this point, they begin to pay particular attention to the main points already extracted in an effort to transfer them into their LTM as described in chapter 7. Having a revision plan written down for an exam is one thing; the actual act of revising the plan is another.

Regardless of the textbooks, revision guides, notes, and hand-outs you might have accrued for studying, if you are not revising efficiently, you are wasting valuable resources. It is paramount to understand how and when to revise. This is because the way you revise for an exam has an impact on memory, retention, and recall of information. The following are some important tips for revision:

- **Read actively.** Some students suffer from poor concentration during reading; their attention span fades after five or ten minutes. This is simply because their brain is not used to reading actively for a longer period of time. With practice, concentration improves and alertness expands. Note that the way you read a textbook is different from the way you read a novel. A novel can be read at leisure—on a train, plane, and generally anywhere. A textbook requires active attention embedded with a sense of time and deadline. Students are therefore encouraged to read with purpose and deadline in mind.
- **Read and study.** Revising and cramming should never be considered the same thing. I remember years back when I ran out of time for a particular exam, and my brain froze. It felt like my brain simply stopped working, as if on strike. My neurons and brain cells felt bunched up and tangled. I simply couldn't recollect anything I had crammed. This was because I made the common mistake of trying to cram all I took note of. Today, when I reread some of my written work from years back, it looks incoherent, poorly organised, boring, and like some sort of bullet-point list. My written work back then had no flow, no consistency, no composure, no thought, just pieces of relevant information placed in irrelevant places.
- **Understanding should take priority at all times.** Students are much more interested in remembering information for the exam than understanding it—especially in subject areas that permit memorisation, like foreign vocabulary, equations, or multiple-choice questions. However, while understanding is assumed to be time-consuming, it is better than memorising or cramming in that it amplifies a broader application of knowledge for better confidence and attaining better marks during an exam. Understanding key topics and subject matter permits each student to not only remember facts they highlighted with a coloured marker in a textbook or class notes—names, formulas, equations—but also to be apply them in a way that not only shows good memory recall but also a distinct flow in answers and a deliberate, concise competence in understanding the subject area and other required questions.
- **Avoid cramming for an exam.** Cramming and memorisation as a means to avoid spending the time to study efficiently tends to be

visible during the marking process and affects your overall grade. Teachers/markers struggle to engage with the written work of students who deal mainly in memorisation or cramming, because that work displays no persuasive quality. It is not cogently organised. There is no flow, and the teacher is continuously interrupted to make sense of the bits they have managed to put together that seem like copy and paste.

General Study Tips

Study tips give you an advantage over other students, as they suggest an efficient method of studying. Some students go through classroom notes and pages and replicate that same information during exams. They fail to apply useful study tips and techniques during the study and revision period and end up doing poorly. Their work typically shows signs of cramming, including lack of coherency in structure, failure to apply relevant facts, and in some cases poor grammar. These are all signs of poor revision, which will be evident in your work when examiners are marking it.

In comparison, high-performing students display in their exams essay competence that includes cogent essay structure and exceptional spelling and grammar. High-performance students don't just work hard; they understand the need for implementing a good study strategy when they learn. Study tips, therefore, should guide you throughout the academic year, through to the exam day.

Before you begin your study, it is suggested that you have a vivid idea of the material you need to study with and what study materials are available to you. To do that, you need to do some research on methods that have proven to be most effective. There are numerous books, websites, and YouTube videos which can be used to give you preference for learning tips. Consider also the following factors that influence your ability to study well.

Motivation

Studying requires a considerable amount of motivation and energy if it is to be effective. Before you begin to study, you should have a sense of motivation. Motivation is a crucial element during the study period. Some students don't feel like studying; they don't feel like giving up what they love to do for what they need to do. They'd rather sit and watch TV or go out at leisure with friends. However, the thought of failing the year, or the sincere desire to finish the year with high marks, usually gives us the right motivation to sit down and put in the hours to study.

Students who want to move on to the next academic year are usually motivated when it comes to revising for their exam. The transition to the next academic stage is usually based on a genuine motivation to finish the year. Completing the year and graduating with your peers is one motivation; making your parents proud or yourself proud is another. For some, getting the job they really want is a powerful motivating factor.

It has been conclusively shown that students who are motivated are more focused and are able to avoid common student distractions. For instance, by being motivated, you can remain alert and focus on your revision while eliminating distractions such as procrastination, being lazy, and partying endlessly.

Friend selection

Peer pressure is often present and places unnecessary stress on the student who needs attention and focus for an upcoming exam. While at times the collaboration with friends during an exam is quite motivating, exciting, and engaging, it can cause a distraction, in particular when what your friends have to say is out of the context of what you have to study at that moment. Unless you have a pack with a similar study mindset, it is better to study alone.

For instance, if you find yourself in a group of students who are studying at a different rate than you or a different subject or question than you, it is best to avoid them during the exam period. They might be ahead of you or behind you in their study, which might put you in a stressful situation whereby you begin to think that you have little to contribute or nothing to contribute or more to contribute than you should. It is therefore advised to assess the situation thoroughly and be selective with who you want as your study pack before the exam day.

Organisation

A study plan is a must for upcoming exams—in particular when you have more than one exam to work on. In the previous chapter, we discussed the relevance of time management and how to apply Exam-SMART principles so that you can stay on track with your studies and revision. A scheduled plan is therefore pivotal. It lays out how you should prioritise your work and how you should divide and distribute your time to ensure that you don't fall behind and can cover all possible ground in your revision promptly.

Social Surroundings

It is not conducive, for example, to study in a crowded place with people yelling and loud music playing. At the very least, it is distracting. Where you study is just as relevant as everything else you have put together for your study and revision period. While you might be adequately prepared to study and revise, if your environment is not study friendly—you have a noisy neighbour, say, or you live in a house where everyone always wants your attention for anything and everything—you will be easily distracted and find concentration challenging to manage.

One possibility would be to study at the library, if you can access one near where you live. Another is to inform anyone who is likely to disturb you not to do so at this particular time. You can get a bit dramatic and creative by making a DO NOT DISTURB sign and hanging it where everyone can see and read it. I prefer to study in a deserted and peaceful environment, away from the crowd, including my friends.

Some students are scared of losing friends because of study. However, if the friends are also productive, they will say, "Okay, while you catch up on this, I will look into that so I can catch up on this" rather than "You need to get your priorities right."

CHAPTER 13

The Practicality Process of Revising

Nothing visualised can materialise until we physically,
strategically, and practically get to work with it.

This chapter focuses on getting practical during the study and revision period. Exam preparation requires implementing a certain revision routine and taking specific practical steps. Generally, for everything we have done, want to do, or can do—even through trial and error—there is always a way to do it and a way to do it better, practically and literally.

Exams have been around for years and practically tested, exploited, and improved by many, leading to a collective experience of successful stories which as a consequence have now resulted in a variety of study guides. For this reason, almost all previous work on exam revision has one thing in common: systematic steps on how to study. What this chapter does is confirm this position and extend it by giving it better transparency.

Tens of thousands of students around the world have specific study rituals that they engage in. Some students certainly have favourite study music, study routines, lucky charm/crucifix, special prayers, study places, food, and friends. This chapter suggests that they will work better with the right study guide. The majority of this chapter will explain in practical steps how to execute your study session systematically and practically.

How Much Time Should Be Spent in Revision?

A common question usually asked by students is, "How much time should I invest in revision?" I would love to give you an accurate answer, a confirmation that says, "Study X amount of hours daily, weekly, or monthly, and you will be fine." However, the truth is, it is all circumstantial and based on individual circumstances. For instance, you might have a part-time job, look after siblings or other family members, or be a slow learner. Other factors might include deadlines before the exam day, how organised your notes are, how many subjects you have to revise for, and the time gap between exams.

Depending on the above factors, you might have to read daily or a few times during each week. This includes the fact that some subjects require more attention—mostly when your current gap in knowledge requires further reading. It could vary from spending a few hours daily on reading to spending hours every few days on reading.

Let's say you have a month to prepare for two exams now. Exam A is due on 29 April, and Exam B is due on 31 April. I would suggest that you spend week 1 on exam B, week 2 on exam A, and then spend half of week 3 on exam B and half on exam A. In week 4, the final week before the exam, spend half the first few days on exam B, then the other half on exam A so it is fresh on your mind before the exam. Once exam A is finished, rest for a few hours, then refresh your memory on exam B before the exam day.

Revision Techniques

Checklist

Students are advised to have control over their study and revision session at all times. Therefore, before we continue, it is worth going over a quick study and revision checklist. Questions to ask before you start include:

- Have you set yourself a SMART study goal for each subject?
- Have you got a study schedule along with time frames and sufficient breaks in between?
- Are your notes written, relevant, and organised?
- Are your study sessions prioritised (always start with the hardest subjects first)?
- Have you got some past papers ready to test yourself later on?

- Is your environment conducive to studying and free of distraction like noise, siblings, friends, and parents?
- Are you actually ready to start your revision (actively revising)?

Be Stationery Equipped

Having the right stationery is relevant to your exam preparation. Without the right tools, getting the job done well can be tricky. It is suggested that students ensure that they have specific stationery in place to aid an active revision session. Some educational institutions provide student with some of the instruments they might need to carry out effective revision. Stationery instruments you should have ready include the following:

- exam year planner
- Tipex for correction
- sufficient pens, such as fluorescent markers and fountain pens
- ruler and/or calculator, depending on the exam subject
- Post-it notes
- ring binders with different sections divided by coloured cards
- A4/A6 plastic file that could be reinserted
- dictionary for difficult or challenging words

Daily Clue (Post-It Notes)

At my desk, I usually have Post-it notes all over the wall regarding two or three different concepts or formulas I would like to remind myself of daily and throughout the week. Each time I pass by, I glance at them, and I read a few of them. After a while, they stick to my brain like those sticky notes.

According to research, the information we store in our brain is transmitted by brain cells called *neurons*, which activate in the hippocampus, a part of the brain responsible for ensuring that data passes from the short-term memory (STM) into the long-term memory (LTM)—definitely an essential part of the brain to look after. Neurons strengthen over time based on how often in succession we repeat or rehearse specific information over and over again.

The act of putting a few critical concepts on a surface where you can easily see them is one way of reinforcing something you don't want to forget. By going over that particular piece of information, i.e., having a sticky Post-it note where you can see it daily and actively and consciously checking up on it, that information will become consolidated in your memory for later fast retrieval.

3 x 5 Index Card Technique

Some students who are great at recollecting facts and concepts take advantage of index cards to organise relevant information into small chunks. This is a beneficial and practical technique used to transfer vital information from the STM into the LTM. The idea is to minimise specific information by putting one or two essential facts or key concepts on one index card. This filters and narrows the focus of the brain on smaller pieces of information for maximum efficiency.

Some student prefers to use one 3 x 5 index card per concept or question. They write a question on one side and the answer on the opposite side, so when they read the question and answer it, they can flip it straight away to see if the answer they thought of was indeed the right one. This technique is more practical and works well when a student has plenty of time to create the cards.

Fact Isolation Technique

There are many factors that affect a student's ability to recollect critical facts and concepts. One of them is overcrowded information. I created a revision study material not long ago called an Exam Revision Notebook for this very purpose. Students spend too much time reading large chunks of information over and over again in an attempt to understand or remember it.

One of my students spends a lot of time highlighting large chunks of text in her textbook—sometimes a whole page—in an attempt to try to understand the content as well as remember all the details. She ends up feeling frustrated because she can't remember half or most of the dates of events, the names of critical concepts, or the meaning behind them in depth. A classmate of mine experienced a similar issue. He struggled to remember principal theories and dates. The dates all looked similar, so they were easy to confuse and mix up. I went through his study notes and found all the relevant information there. However, I noticed one problem: the key facts were crowded by other facts and information.

The problem was not that he had all the answers in front of him or she didn't have the resources to hand or the facts in front of her. Both were drifting and floating away in voluminous information. I told each of them that the best way to learn and remember efficiency is by isolating critical points from the information readily produced. Once your revision note is fully complete on specific subject matter, make it a priority to isolate the key facts away from the rest of the vital information. This way, you can quickly go through smaller chunks of information (the key facts and concepts) at any given time in order to remember them better while at the same time going through all information over again before the actual exam.

Audio

The majority of students listen to music and own a pair of headphones. It is advisable to try to record all lectures and listen to them later—or once your revision is finalised, tape them in your own voice. In most cases, teachers will have covered most of what would come out during the exam, so ensure you tape them in class. I usually use this technique in combination with 3 x 5 index cards and the Exam Revision Notebook.

This is a more relaxed technique. It feels like going through the lecture again in class, over and over again, as if reliving a day as much as you want. At night, when I feel like resting my eyes, I can just lie down and listen to the lecture or my own recording of the information I am trying to understand and remember. This technique is most useful for individual students who prefer to learn through listening.

Study Group

As mentioned earlier in this book, having a study pack has its own advantages. It provides a system through which students can share ideas and opinions with each other before the exam. Some students prefer to study with other people rather than alone. They get bored easily studying by themselves. It is therefore advisable to either find a study group within your subjects or create a study group. You get to hang around with your friends and do something productive together.

Turn Off Your Engine

Some students—and I was one of them—study for a long time. They don't move. They don't stretch. They just sit there, hunched over their books, reading, revising, and highlighting for hours straight. They don't take a break, and as a result, they overwork their brain by bombarding it with old and new information and not giving it sufficient time to process previous revised information. Remember, while your memory is capable of storing a lot of information (endless storage capacity through LTM), it can't function on constant demand. It needs time to cool off. Revising for hours on end doesn't make you any smarter. It just makes you feel fatigued.

When you start feeling fatigued, it becomes harder to concentrate. You begin to feel tired. Your mind starts to wander alongside. You begin to lose interest in what you want to revise. Suddenly, all interest and motivation to carry on are lost. Everything begins to feel harder than it looks, because you are spending energy you don't actually need to spend. Students who fail to take adequate breaks and rest while revising usually end up frustrated, and their marks never reach a top level no matter how hard they may have studied for the exam.

It is suggested that during studies, students should aim to take a thirty to forty-five minute break between forty-five-minute revision sessions. This reduces the burden of studying hard by a notch or two. Also, give yourself a day off between days of studies. You will feel more refreshed when you come back the next day to tackle the revision. Take time out, switch off, go out, get some fresh air, do what you love to do, and have a quick little adventure away from the books.

CHAPTER 14

The Big Day

*The big day is where every student gets a say in
how they want to build their future.*

What all previous chapters have attempted to do is equip you with the necessary skills, study tips, and revision techniques for your exams. At this stage in the book, you should be confident about preparing for your exam. This chapter, therefore, aims to offer you crucial advice on how to approach the actual big day—exam day.

The majority of exam failure, in hindsight, could have been predicted, managed, prevented, avoided, and overcome simply by following the practical steps this book has expanded on right from the very beginning and throughout each chapter. It should now follow that at the end of this chapter, students/readers will have gained advanced knowledge and insight on how to be mentally and physically prepared for the big day. Hopefully, at this point, you are fully equipped with the relevant knowledge and understanding of what you want to know, what you wish to achieve, and how you should perform to attain it. If for one reason or another you are unsure about these, my advice would be to reread the relevant chapters of this book.

In the event of unforeseen circumstances (like health issues or any other reasonable situation) that prevent you from taking the exam, your priority should be to inform the appropriate department as early as possible. Don't leave it to the last minute. However, if all is well with you, you should be ready for exam day.

Exam Day

Students should be aware of specific rules before exam day arrives to avoid common mistakes. Not observing these rules only adds more stress to your day. For instance, you should know the specific rules of conduct for examinations—that candidates should arrive at the exam room ten to twenty minutes before the exam, for example, or candidates should bring and display their institutional ID bearing a visible photo of themselves. A good recommendation is that students should ensure they have taken the proper steps and know all the requirements at least a week before the actual day.

It is not unusual on exam day to find yourself noticeably uneasy despite having done sufficient revision and studied hard. You may feel anxious, panicky, suspenseful, and eager to get the exam behind you so the feeling will go away. Your approach to the actual day is quite an important factor in mitigating these circumstances and at times eliminating them. Therefore, regardless of the above potential situations, how you approach exam day plays a major role in how well you will manage your emotions and nerves.

My second-to-last exam day was nerve-racking! I had done the reading and studied efficiently, but I still found myself full of nerves a day before the exam. But why? I was merely experiencing the natural exam-day stress familiar to most students—the unavoidable fear of the unknown. I managed this well the next day because I undertook specific measured steps.

Give yourself sufficient time to arrive at the designated building for the exam. Students who arrive early have adequate time to control their nerves and reduce their stress level. They have time to rerun concepts in their head calmly and even chat with friends if they so choose.

Arriving ahead of the start time also provides students with a relaxing breathing pace. In an extreme situation, if you are late, you might not be allowed to take the exam, which means that all your effort in revising would go to waste.

Avoid your phone before you sit an exam. It could distract you. Besides, phones are not allowed in the exam room. Students found with their phones are either told to leave the exam room or penalised in other ways.

Avoid participating in conversations that are negative before the exam— like some student arguing a particular question and conflict over the right answer. Before and on the exam day, go through the instructions once again. There might be materials relevant to what you need to bring along with you.

Before the Exam

Listen carefully to the invigilator's instruction as to start time, stop time, break times, code of conduct, etc. Before the exam, depending on the type, you might need specific materials. Ensure that you have asked your teachers/lecturer about what you should bring with you. For instance, during my A-level in maths, there was a particular type of calculator we were allowed to use for the occasion.

Think about your primary objective, which is to answer all required questions as best you can. Your aim should be to do so by producing a well-written exam answer paper. Remember the burden of proof of academic competence at the beginning of this book? This is what you have to display in your written work. The responsibility is now on you as the student to show the competence expected to go to the next academic stage. This is your opportunity to showcase your hard work and prove you have prepared well in advance.

During the Exam

Before you start writing, read all the instructions attached to the exam paper carefully so you know what is expected. The mistake some students make is to rush into the exam question, get halfway through writing, then realise that they are meant to answer the questions in a specific order or specific ways—for example, answer a question from part A and two from part B. Work with your time. Divide it equally among all questions. This gives you an even amount of time to spend on each question rather than focusing too much on one question at the expense of another.

As suggested in previous chapters, achieving a top grade on an exam can be executed by following specific guidelines when answering exam questions. Students should seek to implement the following guidelines when writing their examination answers:

- Read the questions properly. Pay particular attention to what the question is demanding of you.
- Create a mental plan in your head or write an outline of how you want to proceed, if allowed to, somewhere on your exam question

paper. Your outline should include an introduction, evaluation, critique, comparison, contrast, supporting evidence, and conclusion.

- Ensure that each answer is coherently linked, has a consistent flow, and is written in a timely manner. Where applicable, justify your answer in a persuasive way.
- Review your answer one more time before moving on to the next one. Ensure that you have established a sufficient relationship between the question and your answer and that your answer is relevant.
- Move on to the next question. Follow the above guidelines again from the beginning to the end of your answer.

In cases where you feel stuck on a question, leave sufficient room and then continue with the next exam question as usual. Later, go back to the previous question and attempt it again, following the guidelines above.

Never depart from the exam rules and regulations. Under no circumstance should you be tempted to break any of the rules in the code of exam conduct. That only increases the probability of failing and puts you at a disadvantage even when you have sufficiently studied.

It is imperative to stay calm throughout the whole process during your exam; you remember much better in this state of mind. Even if you draw a blank, your brain goes on strike, and your memory disappears briefly, keep calm and think for a few minutes. You will start making sense of things, and your memory will come back to you, provided you have adhered to the tips and techniques in this book.

At the instruction of the invigilator, you may have to cross out any rough working on your exam paper. Remember to do that before you hand your paper in.

Always ensure that your handwriting is legible. Take your time when writing; it has to be readable for marking. There is a difference between neat handwriting and legible handwriting, and there is a difference between both and a scribble that can't be easily deciphered. I understand that we don't all have neat handwriting. I speak for myself here. However, during an exam, make sure your handwriting is at least legible. If you have to write more slowly and deliberately, do so. Important vital points are no good if the markers can't interpret what you have written. Illegible writing might also restrict your flow of rereading your work before handing it in.

After the Exam

Now that you have got through the exam, give yourself a break. Don't panic or sweat over the exam you have taken. It is done. Just get something nice to eat or drink. Do the things you have disciplined yourself not to do because you have put them all aside and prioritised your revision and studies over them. Do something fun, something adventurous, something less stressful but joyful. You made it!

CHAPTER 15

Making Sense of Education

Education is the foundation of our very existence, for it is that which fills the curious lives of mankind. It is in our nature as humans to crave knowledge, to crave experience, to crave power, to crave advancement, to crave understanding, to crave justification, to crave certainty, to crave friendship, to crave culture, to connect and understand them all, and then to distribute them proudly among one another like a treasure unearthed over and over again, from generation to generation, from century to century.

This is a useful chapter for students who are struggling to ascribe meaning and value to what education can provide in return for their commitment and engagement. This chapter suggests that education in any country, in any era, in any evolution, and in any revolution is the most powerful asset that individuals can acquire throughout their lifespan.

Today, education is treated with a sense of feared distance, like something dusty, old, and ancient; like something antique that belongs to a galleria or museum, for display only; like something that should be admired from a distance and never approached from the inside. But why? This chapter seeks to make sense of education and give it a new spotlight. After giving education objective value and meaning, it goes on to propose a connection between education and exams, and that students can derive various life skills from education and taking exams.

Over the years, the concept of education has been diluted and diminished, with all sort of negative connotations and excuses attached to it. Student often express themselves with great exasperation, loathing, and frustration when faced with a conflict about what they want, what education can do for them, or what education has not done for others. They say things like:

- "Look at John. He has a degree, but he is in debt, and he has not found a proper job."
- "Is there any point in me being here?"
- "I don't want to end up with debt after university."
- "Education is boring and not for me."
- "I didn't like my institution, my teacher, or my classmates."
- "I am making some money now, which is better than sitting in a class that doesn't interest me."

For most of my educational life, I never thought about what education was. Growing up, like countless other students, I thought that education was mainly about schooling, about qualification, about getting the right job to earn more money than my peers. Generally, it has been a reinforced ideal in our era that education is about getting a better job and making money. When students fail to acquire this promised prize at the end of their education, they feel lied to and cheated by the educational system.

I began to write this chapter on a grey, cloudy, rainy day after one of my master's lectures. Because I had no umbrella with me, I headed for the city library, one close to my lecture building. I sat close to a window, at first staring at empty space. Then I watched the windows attacked by raindrops. Each drop landed forcefully before crawling down the window.

I turned my attention to my fellow students' movements as they went about their individual business: some in deep thought, some reading, some flipping through pages, some rearranging loose papers, some chatting in packs, some texting, some giggling, others laughing, pecking away on their keyboards. I began to ponder many questions:

- What is education?
- What is so special about education?
- Why is it so curiously craved?
- Why does it seem so necessary, so required, so crucial, and so essential?

These are the questions I felt obliged to ponder, to discuss, to answer, to express, to write down, and to share.

I began by defining education. I came to the conclusion that education is an expansive tool that consists of crucial accumulation of information and instruction, established over time through decades, and delivered by the informed and instructed to the uninformed for the benefit of general human awareness, advancement, achievement, refinement, maintenance, unity, and the personally acquisition of knowledge, habits, skills, beliefs, status, innovation, and power. Education is exclusively inclusive, a single powerhouse containing everything we humans crave to acquire in our lifespan.

According to Francis Bacon, "Knowledge is power." I believe this brief statement to be one of the most powerful in human history. If one looks closely, education is the single most crucial connection between humans and existence. It is a consensus that binds the whole world together; a global language of value, respect, and shared history. Without education, purpose dies, meaning fades, morality diminishes, disadvantage increases, death multiplies, poverty grows, and the balance of power tilts permanently to one side, regardless of the nation and irrespective of the era.

As humans, it is in our nature to crave knowledge. Our instinct is to test boundaries, and our desire is to explore conclusions and advance them further. Because of this, we lean towards learning, towards education. We come in search of meaning, of facts, of values, of evidence, of ourselves. Education is the essence of human craving. It is that which encourages us to exploit creativity, to predict outcomes, to identify opportunity, to erect success, to avoid error, to save time, to accept peace, to maintain health, to anticipate consequences, and to navigate conclusions, no matter who we are, and no matter which country we live in.

It should follow that while education is mostly ascribed to an academic institution, it extends outside of academia. Education is required to analyse the accuracy of events, to address crucial political and moral decisions, to dismiss ambitious arguments, to increase morals, to set boundaries, to eliminate prejudice, to propose a solution, and to justify current and future predictions. Education is simply the summary of these natural intentions. We as humans seek knowledge through education because we want to advance in life and improve our living conditions. Education is the safeguard of prehistorical activities and the advancement of continuous evolution. Without education, human history will be lost alongside human significance, human achievement, and human potential.

Making Further Sense of Exams

"Is there really a need for an exam?" a student asked me one day.

I said yes and went on to give various reasons why exams are relevant: to test knowledge; to ensure competence to move on to the next stage; to achieve a degree; to explore strength and weaknesses; and to address gaps in knowledge. But is that all? I felt that it was not.

I thought that there must be something more to the examining of students in education. I began to think, ponder, and debate various plausible answers. I concluded that exams exist to maintain compliance and increase advancement of knowledge delivered through education. Exams are the guardians of information. Education is based on the accumulation of experienced knowledge which is based on information gathered, studied, and delivered over time. Accuracy must be maintained during the transition from information to knowledge.

Knowledge consists primarily of experience gained through the search and acquisition of profound, validated, and relevant information, which is then delivered through the method of teaching and examination. Conclusively, education is a combination of acquired experience and knowledge through information that must come under scrutiny. Diligent care should be taken here, because a prerequisite to gathering information is that it must be accurate, transparent, consensus, and established without bias. The information required for the purpose of knowledge must undergo scrutiny to ensure accuracy, transparency, validity, and respect. It must be comply with established knowledge and in sync with previous facts as they are known.

The Link Between Education and Exams

Various chapters in this book have discussed the purpose of taking an exam. It is suggested that exams exist so students can showcase a distinctive level of knowledge and understanding—for example, through showing proof of competence, proof of having what it takes to move on to the next academic or career stage, and proof of confidence in attained knowledge. But is that all?

Remember that education is about advancement, betterment, history, and evolution. It must be delivered accurately, transparently, factually and respectfully. Apart from testing individual students' competence in the acquisition of knowledge, exams also ensure that diligent care has been taken and that individual students can reproduce knowledge factually, transparently, accurately, and respectfully when required to do so.

Accuracy of Information

The information learned has to be accurate in the sense that it has not been diverted or diluted from what it should be. The information should be referenced and traced to an established source, one that is based on readily available proof. Students should be able to check and verify the information upon request.

Transparency of Information

The information learned must not be ambiguous. It must be straight and clear and void of bias. A teacher or student should be able to get the gist of the information quickly, whenever or wherever they come across it. This ensures that facts remain facts when they are being delivered in the form of teaching or training and upon reproduction on exams.

Relevance of Information

The difficulty so far for students is to ascertain which information is relevant for the purpose of exam write-up. Information is growing at full speed and crowding all other pieces of information. Students should, therefore, pay particular attention when obtaining information. Focus on quality over quantity. If it is not relevant, it is not necessary.

Using the wrong information for the right project, for example, leads to a bad outcome. A piece of information that lacks relevance is worthless and hinders education. Each piece of information has to be scrutinised and assessed for suitability. Is this information relevant for the purpose for which it is needed? Information is usually created for a specific purpose. Facts have value in one area and none in others.

Compliance of Information

Each piece of information retrieved for academic or training purposes must be in compliance with certain rules, expressed or implied. For instance, it must be established that the information has integrity and has not been compiled based on a lie or a false belief. There must be supporting evidence showing that the information is factual and has evidence supporting it. All academic information must comply with the source it is taken from.

A common strategy is to cite well-established authors or a well-known source to support a piece of information. Teachers and student are required to prove that the information they have is in compliance, can be verified, and is in fact correct.

Developing Opportunities through Exams and Education

An opportunist is someone who sees fruitfulness in something and focuses on obtaining it. As students, we are opportunistic about a future outside of academia. We need education to travel prepared into the future. We crave knowledge and seek information because we want to take our living standards a step further. We wish to acquire knowledge so we can utilise it to our advantage later for the purpose of better living for ourselves and others.

Education is a powerful tool and should be used with caution, expertise, intelligence, professionalism, care, respect, dignity, and a sense of accountability. To comply with these implied requirements, an exam is highly relevant, required, and useful. Remember, education is the acquisition of knowledge through information for the purpose of human awareness, advancement, achievement, refinement, maintenance, and unity, and the personal acquisition of knowledge, habits, skills, beliefs, status, innovation, and power.

The act of taking an exam ensures that relevant skills are reproducible in at least the same way that they have been taught. An exam is a scrutinising tool which maintains the accuracy, transparency, relevance, and respect of information derived for the purpose of obtained knowledge. Without such a tool, we might lose the origin and originality of information. We might misrepresent the facts and dilute critical knowledge through wrongful information at the detriment of human existence and advancement.

Education exposes us to an environment where we can practice the adaptation of new and significant skills which are not readily available outside academia. Even in a disadvantaged society, education prevails, for it is understood as the best available way to turn a disadvantaged society into an advantaged one. Opportunistic students understand that there is knowledge to be derived from education for the benefit of society. Consequently, they pursue it. They attempt to acquire it for the purpose of advancement: academically, personally, socially, and economically.

That is why we are all gathered in the amphitheatre room numerous days a week, listening attentively, making skilful scribbles, staying alert and engaged, watching every move of our teachers/lecturers, listening to their voices, forming arguments in our heads, forming opinions and perspectives. We then go to the library in search of more information, looking through loose papers, articles, textbooks, and the library PC, eyes darting at the monitor screen, clicking curiously, craving answers. We are opportunists. We are students. That is what we are supposed to do.

In the process of this weekly repetition, we inevitably form practical skills and competence. We then go on to reproduce that competence in our exams. At this stage, students should begin to notice that the overall demand for exams propels students to be better equipped and provides them with the opportunity to develop various skills, such as the ability to do the following:

- research and examine facts and opinions
- evaluate information and form a better judgement in the process
- be independent in finding answers to questions
- propose a persuasive answer after careful examination
- compare, contrast, and distinguish between information that is necessary and information that is not
- follow specific instructions and comply with specific requirements
- demonstrate attentiveness to detail and show a special kind of recollection when required to reproduce it
- show genuine organisational skills relevant in all area of life
- anticipate and predict common answers to common problems
- interpret concepts, information, and facts in a new unique voice
- be ready for the expectations outside academia

Education and Personal Living through Exams and Education

Education is not for everyone, but students should be aware that, while we don't have to be educated to be successful in life, success cannot survive without an educated mind. Moreover, in a competitive world like today's, education is what makes each individual more readily competitive and better equipped to deal with sudden life changes, various business activities, and innovative changes.

Apart from moral guidance, one of the first serious conversations about the future that our parents or guardians have with us is about education—whether it concerns preschool, college, or university. This is because our parents and guardians want us to be the very best we can be and extend to us the dream they maybe couldn't attain. Our parents and our government understand the power of education in everyone's life. For instance, our parents might say, "If you want to become somebody in life, you need to go to school, study, learn, and get the grades in." They are right! All parents want to see their kids become happy and prosperous, and we as children and students want to make our parents proud.

Generally, as humans, we want so many things in life. In no particular order, we might wish to have good health, money, love, wealth, stability, and higher status. To achieve these economic or personal goals, we need to think about how they can be achieved and how they can realistically be applied to our lives. Apart from academic achievements and skills, education helps us face the challenges of life, manage unexpected events, manage failure, or avoid failure altogether. In addition, knowledge gives us the chance to reap the rewards of other people's experiences through reading, books, papers, and listening to videos/seminars presented by people who have gone through it all. Education keeps us immune from hopelessness, idleness, and regretful failures. And while failure is brought about by lack of foresight—either through unforeseen circumstances or neglect—it is sustained by lack of education.

In my first book, *My Student Pledge Journal*, I suggested that education is what enabled certain prominent individuals to attain the level of recognition and achievement they have attained today, including former US president Barack Obama, former UK prime minister David Cameron, former Taiwanese president Ma Ying-Jeou, and Russian president Vladimir Putin. Other prominent educated individuals include the following:

- Ethiopian prime minister Hailemariam Desalegn Boshe
- Australian prime minister Tony Abbott of Australia
- Austrian president Heinz Fischer
- Indian prime minister Manmohan Singh
- author JK Rowling
- author Caroline Kepnes
- author John Grisham
- author Stephen King
- actor Gerard Butler
- actor James Franco
- celebrity Sir David Attenborough
- actress Rachel Maddow
- actor David Tennant
- sportsman Andy Murray
- actor Ken Jeong
- actor Masi Oka
- actor David Duchovny
- actress Sigourney Weaver

- actress Lupita Nyong'o
- actress Naomi Campbell
- actor Bradley Cooper
- actor Hill Harper
- actress Mayim Bialik
- actor Vinnie Jones

It is undoubtedly true that wherever you want to get to, education can take you there. Without education, I would never be able to expand on my vision to influence the perspective of my students. Education touches on the economic, social, political, and cultural issues of each country. Education brings about a calibre that is distinct. Education is something we cannot avoid, directly or indirectly. We are all affected by its involvement.

In conclusion, education is not just about the curriculum, libraries, school uniforms, impressive academic reports, textbooks, wooden chairs and desks, blackboards and chalk, schoolbag, pen and paper, and homework. Education goes beyond the four walls of academia. It is not confined to a specific place. It can be acquired everywhere and anywhere, through anyone and everyone. Academia just happens to be one of the most suitable places to learn.

In effect, education is about establishing commitment, facing challenges, defeating obstacles, forming self-identity, unfolding competence, creating and bonding with friends, building confidence, becoming an adult, satisfying expectations, and awakening a new sense of belief in ourselves and others. Furthermore, it balances power, dilutes poverty, encourages advancement, and puts our country in an attractive spotlight for students to want to come over and study.

CHAPTER 16

Quotes to Take on Your Academic Journey

*The desire to carry on and finish is strongly driven
by the motivation that is readily available and
relatively applicable at any giving time.*

Apart from the desire to write educational books and novels, I have developed a genuine deep passion for writing inspirational quotes. Over the years, I have admired written quotes from leading minds such as Albert Einstein, Aristotle, John Dewey, Benjamin Franklin, Malcolm X, Nelson Mandela, Anthony J. D'Angelo, John Hersey, Oprah Winfrey, Jim John, Les Brown, and Abraham Maslow. Today, I develop my own words of wisdom through consistent learning and a constant search for more experience through making the most of each daily encounter.

It is profoundly true that students are the saviours of education, history, and revolution, for without them education cannot be carried on, advanced, or accounted for. I have written several quotes and shared the best ones in books and on social platforms, where I have received unbelievable likes and appreciative comments over the years. These quotes have really helped me through my academic, social, and personal journey in life, and it is apparent that I have not just reached others but touched their hearts and minds in their own life journey.

In all honesty, the academic journey is never smooth. The path at times is filled with potholes that slow the acquisition of knowledge and restrict our capacity to progress as we realistically should. At times, the journey becomes confusing, tedious, and overwhelming. I have also had to conquer various academic barriers to get to where I am today. It is true, as Aristotle puts it, that "the roots of education are bitter, but the fruit is sweet". What he is saying is that the educational road is not smoothly paved; instead, it is wrinkled with creases and filled with potholes we must pass over while striving to reach the finish line.

To achieve our various academic objectives—the marks, degrees, and wonderful experiences that come with learning that money simply can't compensate for—we must find ways to stay motivated, engaged, and committed to our objective, our interest, and our passion, whatever they might be.

I hope you can find within this list of quotes one that will resonate with you and guide you through the difficult times you may encounter on your way to achieving your main academic or personal objectives. This chapter contains useful quotes I have written over a period of time to help people all over the world find meaning in their daily existence and get through the day. I hope to help you wake up with the right level of energy and motivation to pursue your dreams and goals with a determined zeal, meaning, and passion.

In my student quote book, I explained that inspirational quotes are primarily made up of productive thinking and valuable life experiences. The beauty in a quote is its ability to wake the inner belief and confidence in each one of us. As students on a journey to uncover our talent in a world that demands newness in creativity and individuality, we can surely find a companion in quotes. For these reasons, I have included some of my most excellent inspirational quotes here.

- Preparation is the shortest route to getting ahead, staying ahead, and finishing ahead.
- Start your day with creativity and end it with productivity. Creativity is where experience manifests, while productivity is where experience materialises.
- Education is the overall conclusion of the experience we have paid tentative attention to in the process of available opportunity to learn.
- You can't delegate good grades. You have got to put in the work to get the worth.

- Don't let your circumstance dictate your competence, your movement, or your sanity.
- Education is a bargain when it comes to success, for it is filled with fruitful results that money can't fully compensate for.
- To do better you have to know better. This is where knowledge and understanding come into play.
- If you want something bad enough, you will go out of your way well enough.
- Fear of failure does not stop failure; it only prolongs solution.
- If you are not doing what you love, you are afraid of something. Figure it out, and you are halfway there. Get rid of it, and you are about to experience the start of a better life.
- When you know what you want and believe in yourself, no amount of criticism can stop you.
- Even if others say you can't do it, it is their words against your actions, and actions speak louder.
- If you make yourself the last person to quit on you, you will never have the chance to.
- Family is not defined by blood but by love.
- Genius is a combination of creativity and craziness.
- Quitting is not on the menu today, tomorrow or the day after.
- Every day is an unspoken invitation to lead a successful life.
- Our achievement is what we are known by. Our commitment is what we are understood by.
- Knowledge is the most powerful weapon designated to humanity.
- Knowledge is direction.
- You don't have to understand it the first time. Just don't make the first time the last time you try to.
- You are your getaway ticket.
- They told me that I was incapable of doing it, and I told them they were incapable of stopping me.
- If you can't finish it today, don't lose sleep over it. Lose worry instead. Tomorrow is another complete day.
- Want to know more? Read more. Books reveal the infinite capabilities of humankind and the endless extension of the world we've always known.
- If you can visualise it, you can materialise it.
- You don't have to be educated to be successful. But success can't survive without an educated mind.
- Understanding is the beginning of progress.
- Don't be distracted by problems; be attracted by solutions.

- In life, you need two kinds of income: one to pay your bills, another to pave your future.
- Only when your philosophy starts changing for the better will your ideas start expanding for the best.
- It is your job to make you happy.
- Keep believing in what you do, because the only thing that matters and the everything that matters is that. It does not have to mean anything to anybody; it just has to mean everything to you.
- If you are tired or edgy, don't delete everything. Don't throw in the towel. Put it all away in your come-back box and do something you enjoy without effort. Then come back to it and tackle it with a fresh you.
- To get ahead in life, you have to show a different kind of bravado.
- The odds are never against you. It is just the fear of feeling inadequate to compete.
- All students deserve an education they can learn to earn with.
- Movement is taking a step each day. Progress, however, is taking each day a step.
- Imagination is the product of a relentless deep desire, filled with a vivid longing to explore new possibilities regardless of any real or potential risk or danger.
- Every now and then, do some personal chores, like decluttering your social atmosphere. Life is too short to be shared with negative people.
- Never be too busy to dream, and never be too idle to act.
- Circumstance and change go hand in hand, like a pencil and an eraser. If circumstance becomes a mistake, simply erase them with a change.
- Certain things require giving 100 per cent to achieve them, and that we might not have. The key to remember is that if you give your current all, your best effort, whatever that might be, your per cent will certainly, definitely, and eventually grow into the required 100 per cent for the job.
- Make each second a story worth telling.
- We are accountable to lead the change we dream to see.
- Inspiration is the seed of creativity.
- Never forget that success or failure is a matter of discretion, not destiny.
- Nothing is far-fetched; you just have to want it more than you wish it.

- Sometimes just thinking outside the box isn't sufficient. You have to step outside of and away from the box, then think.
- Impossibility is a myth.
- If you start your day with a plan, your day will start following the direction you have envisaged in your mind.
- Growth requires a combination of criticism and praise.
- Failure is an opportunity to reaffirm your determination to succeed.
- There is never a shortage of talented individuals, just a shortage of self-belief and confidence.
- Start the way you are, but don't stay the way you came.
- You dominate when you win, gain more when you fail, but lose all if you quit.
- Talent is the equivalent of wings. Want to fly? Use yours.
- The world is full of opportunities. Don't let the odds overrule your chance to excel.
- If you wake up today without a goal or a dream, it simply means you've missed out on yesterday's opportunity.
- Start with the end in plan and watch the plan end as you started.
- You are not obliged to accept your circumstance. If you don't like it, change it.
- Everyone needs support. Don't push away the people who are determined to be yours.
- Learning is the foundation of transformation.
- The moment you start taking your ideas further, they start taking you further.
- Always keep a journal. Nothing important should go un-captured and un-written down.
- Accountability is not an obligation but a contribution: a contribution of your finest effort in reaching your finest result.
- Don't let the everyday burden distract you from the everyday possibilities.
- Feedback and acceptance drive us forward. Pride and ignorance pull us backwards.
- Don't be fooled into believing or thinking that you weren't born to win.
- Don't be worried about making mistakes. Be worried about missing the opportunity of not encountering them.
- Don't wait for a miracle. Start an idea.
- Don't place a lean budget on your effort. You only produce what you have contributed.
- We are all born to inspire, not just to be inspired.

- Behind every successful person is a student who refused to accept mediocrity.
- The acquisition of all levels of success is temporal. Education is what extends their duration.
- Gratitude is like a boomerang. It always comes back to you if you get the spin right.

CHAPTER 17

Revision Organiser Table

Staying ahead does not require any special talent or skill; it only requires forward planning and preparation through organisation, for organisation is what extends the proximity of a deadline.

Subject	
Due Date	
Start Revision by	
Finish Revision by	

Subject	
Today number of days spent	

Subject	
Due Date	
Start Revision by	
Finish Revision by	
Today number of days spent	
Subject	
Due Date	

Subject	
Start Revision by	
Finish Revision by	
Today number of days spent	

Subject	
Due Date	
Start Revision by	
Finish Revision by	
Today number of days spent	

Subject	
Subject	
Due Date	
Start Revision by	
Finish Revision by	
Today number of days spent	

Subject	
Due Date	
Start Revision by	
Finish Revision by	

Subject	
Today number of days spent	
Subject	
Due Date	
Start Revision by	
Finish Revision by	
Today number of days spent	

Subject	
Due Date	
Start Revision by	

Subject	
Finish Revision by	
Today number of days spent	
Subject	
Due Date	
Start Revision by	
Finish Revision by	
Today number of days spent	

Once again, a special thanks to all my readers and supporters. Whoever you are, wherever you are, I am deeply grateful.

For more inspirational quotes, follow me on Instagram at samson.o.yung. Finally, watch out for my debut novel: my first official fiction novel.

Lightning Source UK Ltd.
Milton Keynes UK
UKHW010046170223
417092UK00012B/679/J